TWAYNE'S WORLD AUTHORS SERIES

A Survey of the World's Literature

Sylvia E. Bowman, Indiana University

GENERAL EDITOR

CANADA

Joseph Jones, University of Texas at Austin

EDITOR

Peter McArthur

TWAS 363

Peter McArthur

Peter McArthur

By ALEC LUCAS
McGill University

TWAYNE PUBLISHERS
A DIVISION OF G. K. HALL & CO., BOSTON

Library of Congress Cataloging in Publication Data

Lucas, Alec.
 Peter McArthur.

   (Twayne's world authors series; TWAS 363: Canada)
   Bibliography: pp. 179–81
   Includes index.
   1. McArthur, Peter, 1866–1924.
PR9199.3.M275Z75   818'.4'09   75–8823
ISBN 0–8057–6214–0

For Coula

Contents

About the Author

Alec Lucas holds degrees from Queen's University, Kingston, Ontario, and from Harvard University, where he received a Ph.D. in 1951. He lived and worked on a farm for many years. Later he taught in both rural and high schools, did fisheries research, and lectured on conservation for the Ontario Department of Planning and Development. Since 1957, Dr. Lucas has been a professor of English at McGill University. A former editor of the Bulletin of the Humanities Association of Canada, he has long been associated with the study of Canadian literature and has spoken and written extensively on it. His recent books on the subject are *Hugh MacLennan*, *The Best of Peter McArthur*, and *Great Canadian Short Stories*.

Preface

Peter McArthur is Canada's most eloquent spokesman for an age that has gone, for that age when the nation passed from the pioneer and agrarian to the modern and industrial. Week in and week out from 1909 to 1924 he made that period the subject of almost everything he said or wrote—of public lectures, poems, stories, unpublished novels, magazine articles, and hundreds of newspaper columns. Sometimes he warned against the dangers to the rural world of urban infiltration and domination, and tilted against technological progress with its gadgets and machines, especially the newfangled automobile. Sometimes he inveighed against politicians and businessmen when they denied farmers' rights and threatened the economy of the agricultural community. Essentially an affirmer, McArthur preferred often to turn to the past to celebrate the accomplishments and values of the early settlers of Ontario, not as ancestor worshiper, but as historian of what he assumed to be the only Canadian tradition. McArthur's prime theme centers, however, in the rural life of his own time. In the country, man lived close to nature, enjoying its beauties, benefiting from its restfulness, and working in harmony with its dynamic forces. There the simple life remained possible, and McArthur never tired of advocating a return to the farm nor of upholding rural ideals as a solution to the problems growing out of modernity.

Much of this kind of defense of the past can be and has been dismissed as old-fashioned or as agrarian myth. Admittedly, McArthur tended to romanticize his subject. He himself had grown up on a pioneer farm. He looked back longingly on his youth, and certainly nostalgia does color his depiction of the past. But he lived his dream and returned to the farm to become a kind of Canadian Cobbett, proclaiming faith in the family, in the home, and in the land, and at the same time damning rural banks as the cat's-paws of high finance operating with the tacit consent of big government. Like Cobbett, too, McArthur advocated change, but such change that, instead of obliterating the past, would preserve it, reviving the spirit of the horse and buggy days when the pace was slow and good neighborliness was a central social policy.

All these matters, from McArthur's concern with gardening to his love of the spirit of nature, constitute the central body of his work as writer. Accordingly, the largest section of this book examines in detail what McArthur wrote about rural life and tries to define the stand he took in describing it.

On one level he was entirely practical in his "back-to-the-land movement." This approach was economic and therapeutic in nature. On another level McArthur's espousal of agrarianism was a protest in the name of value. As an environmentalist himself, he feared that city ideals would displace the traditional and humanistic ideals of the country and lead to depersonalization and alienation within the community. Urban society had already neglected what he termed the home dream for the dream of wealth. McArthur was right to make his stand. He argued for an old-fashioned social theory, but it was based on a myth only inasmuch as idealism is always based on "myth." McArthur was arguing for an approach to living that is still significant but that must be restated continually in a constant battle against a present and increasing materialism. He was trying to demonstrate by the example of his own way of life and convince by statement that the traditional values of Canada were viable.

Although McArthur gained renown as a man who lived the life of a farmer and who chatted about it in a delightful manner in his essays and articles, the chapters that precede "Country Stuff" and that consider his career before his return to Ekfrid in 1908, after twenty years in the world's biggest cities, clearly indicate that a man of letters stood behind farmer McArthur. It was no mere stroke of luck that he wrote the first Canadian pastoral, as Brandon Conron defines the essays on rural life, and that these essays are among the finest in Canadian literature. He achieved his success, not as an untutored genius, but as a man who had spent long years of apprenticeship, so far unexamined in our literary history, as jokesmith, poet, story writer, novelist *manqué,* critic, editor, and free-lancer. The purpose of the earlier sections of this book is, then, to study the literary background from which the "Country Stuff" sprang, for McArthur's essays, or more precisely *causeries,* are the work of a sensitive and intelligent man and a gifted artist. Long practice as a writer made it possible for him to adapt his powers as conversationalist to paper without losing the spontaneity, immediacy, and vitality associated with voice and gesture, and so to turn chatting into an art form.

During recent years McArthur has regained recognition as one of Canada's best humorists, appearing in two distinguished contemporary anthologies of Canadian writing. So far no particular study of his humor has been made. Consequently there is a gap in the history of Canadian literature, and it is this gap that the chapters on humor and on Leacock and the sections on *To Be Taken With Salt* and McArthur's satiric verse, "Cap and Bells," attempt to fill.

Acknowledgments

This book has been made possible largely through a grant from the Canada Council and a sabbatical leave from McGill University. I am grateful also to the following people for information of various kinds bearing on McArthur's life: Mr. W. Eggleston, Mr. J. P. Haskett, Mrs. Daniel McArthur and her husband, the late Daniel McArthur. I wish, also, to acknowledge my debt to Professor D. Cole, who kindly and painstakingly read the manuscript of this book, and to thank those who helped at the Central Library, Toronto, the library at the University of New Brunswick, and the Redpath Library at McGill University.

I acknowledge with thanks the courtesy of those who granted me permission to quote from Peter McArthur's work—the *Globe and Mail*, Toronto, for excerpts from the *Globe;* J. M. Dent & Sons (Canada) Limited, for those from *Familiar Fields, In Pastures Green,* and *The Red Cow and Her Friends;* Hodder & Stoughton, for those from *Around Home* and *Friendly Acres;* the Canadian Publishers McClelland and Stewart, Limited, Toronto, for a passage from *Farmer Premier,* by E. C. Drury; Thomas Allen & Son, Limited, for those from *The Affable Stranger* and *The Last Law—Brotherhood;* the University of Toronto Press for those from *Literary History of Canada;* and Mr. Wahl for those from *A Chant of Mammonism.*

Mr. J. L. Haines graciously permitted me to use material from William Arthur Deacon's papers and from Deacon's book, *Peter McArthur.* Finally Peter McArthur, executor of the McArthur estate, most generously gave me access to all the McArthur papers and the privilege of quoting freely from both printed and manuscript material.

Chronology

1866   Peter Gilchrist McArthur born, March 10, the youngest of a family of three girls and four boys, at the Ekfrid Township homestead, in Middlesex County, Ontario.

1878   McArthur passes the High School Entrance Examinations.

1879   McArthur attends Wardsville High School and then Strathroy Collegiate, but withdraws because of ill health and lack of funds.

1880–   McArthur lives and works on the home farm and writes
1885   poetry, all of which he later destroys.

1884   McArthur's father dies, leaving Peter twenty-five acres of the family farm.

1885   McArthur mortgages his twenty-five acres and reenters Strathroy Collegiate, where he meets and becomes a close friend of Duncan McKellar.

1887   Graduating from Strathroy Collegiate, McArthur enters Strathroy Model School and, after one term (September to December), receives a Public School Teacher's Third Class Certificate.

1888   After six months teaching elementary school at Caradoc, McArthur enters the University of Toronto. He begins submitting jokes to *Grip*.

1889   McArthur quits the University of Toronto to take a job as reporter with the *Mail*.

1890–   Leaving Toronto, McArthur becomes a free-lance writer
1895   in New York. He meets C. Bowyer Vaux, who becomes a lifelong friend and correspondent.

1895   McArthur is appointed editor in chief of the magazine *Truth,* and on September 11, marries Miss Mabel Clara Haywood-Waters of Niagara-on-the-Lake.

1897   Resigning as editor of *Truth* in July, McArthur takes up free-lancing again. Daniel Carman, a son, is born.

1899 McArthur moves to Amityville, Long Island, where he and Jay Hambidge work on a new theory of aesthetics.

1900 A second son, Peter McKellar, is born.

1902 McArthur and family go to England. McArthur contributes the first of eight articles to *Punch*.

1903 A daughter, Kathryn Elizabeth, is born. McArthur works with W. T. Stead on the *Review of Reviews* and the *Daily Paper* and becomes a charter member of the Ends of the Earth Club in New York.

1904 Back in New York, McArthur opens an advertising agency. The McArthurs live in Montclair, New Jersey.

1905 A third son, James Frederick, is born.

1907 The McArthurs move to Niagara-on-the-Lake.

1908 Ian Stuart McArthur born. McArthur acts as public relations man for the Liberal party.

1909 Leaving Niagara-on-the-Lake, the McArthur family moves to the old McArthur homestead. McArthur publishes his first article in the *Globe* on May 29.

1910 The magazine *Ourselves* appears but ceases in 1912, after eight numbers. McArthur begins publishing in the *Farmer's Advocate*.

1911 McArthur is struck and almost killed by a train. He begins a series of articles attacking railway companies.

1913 McArthur appears before the Committee on Banking and Commerce in Ottawa.

1916 McArthur visits Ottawa to discuss questions of public policy with Sir Wilfrid Laurier. He gives his first lecture in his short career as a public lecturer.

1917 The Greater Production Committee is organized largely at McArthur's instigation.

1918 Six thousand farmers in Ottawa hear McArthur speak on farm production and the "folly of new drafts from the farm workers."

1919 On assignment for the *Globe*, McArthur makes a six-week tour of Western Canada. United Farmers ask him to become leader.

1920 McArthur spends a month in the United States gathering material for *The Affable Stranger*.

Chronology

1921   Bliss Carman's poetry reading tour in Canada is organized and managed by McArthur.

1922   McArthur becomes a provisional director of the Ontario Equitable Trust Corporation.

1924   McArthur dies on October 28, following surgery.

Introduction: The Man from Ekfrid

Peter McArthur (the elder) and Catherine McLennan growing up in the Scottish Highlands could scarcely have dreamed that one day they would migrate to Canada where they would meet and marry and become the parents of a son who would make a name as one of Canada's leading men of letters in the early part of the twentieth century.[1] Yet all came to pass. They went to Canada to live on farms in Ekfrid Township in Western Ontario, where they married and begot a son, Peter, who did win fame as a writer, but whose first twenty years were largely an affair of plough and ax.[2] The Scottish tradition of learning was strong in him, and he at last abandoned those tools for book and pen and went to model school, where he received a teacher's certificate and soon afterward an appointment as teacher in a one-room rural school.

It was a big step from a job as teacher in a rural school in 1887 to a position as editor in chief of a big New York magazine, *Truth*, only eight years later, and by 1903, in London, to that of advertising manager of William T. Stead's latest experiment in publishing, the *Daily Paper*. Yet these are the accomplishments of McArthur's early years when he had determined to make his way in the world of letters. Not all, however, had been smooth sailing. In New York his beginnings were most humble, and he made a bread-and-cheese—and beer—living by grinding out jokes for *Judge, Life, Town Topics,* and several other similar publications then catering to the contemporary craze for humor. Besides, the editorship of *Truth* lasted little more than two years before McArthur resigned in a huff in 1897.

Ever an enthusiast, he was soon involved in a new venture, in Amityville, Long Island, where he and his wife and infant son had moved in 1899 to join another Canadian outlander and artist-journalist, Jay Hambidge (January 13, 1867 to January 20, 1924), who had done much work for *Truth* during McArthur's regime.[3] The two men were to write and illustrate a series of

19

humorous sketches on mathematics for *Life*. They went high-brow, however, Hambidge formulating the aesthetics of dynamic symmetry, and McArthur, after the hectic days of free-lancing and the row with *Truth*, pouring out his spiritual turmoil in a sonnet sequence that later was to make up the bulk of *Lines* (1901) and *The Prodigal and Other Poems* (1907), though he managed to find some relief in amateur theatricals at Amityville.[4] Then he was off to England to edit a magazine aimed at dis-seminating the Amityville pronouncements on Greek architecture and sculpture and the mathematical principles of beauty. The journal proved abortive. The two men quarreled. McArthur turned to advertising and writing again. He published a few pieces in *Punch* and a strange and now very rare book, *To Be Taken With Salt: Being an Essay on Teaching One's Grandmother to Suck Eggs* (1903), a social satire that snapped at English, American, and Canadian alike.

The vicissitudes of fortune sat heavily on McArthur in Eng-land. His attempts to prove himself as a businessman with Stead's paper and as an author gained him little; the publisher went broke, and the newspaper failed almost immediately it began. McArthur, chastened by his experiences, returned to the shelter of New York, where, determined to establish himself in business he soon opened an advertising agency. The depression of 1906–1907 closed its doors and drove McArthur back to his boyhood home in an effort to find security. Although he prided himself on being an "idea man" capable of developing surefire advertisements for commercial houses, few clients called on him to assist in "puffing" their merchandise, and about all that came of the undertaking were three booklets of fiction, now extremely rare Canadiana, *The Ghost and the Burglar* (1905), for manu-facturers of locks, *The Peacemakers* (1905), for manufacturers of door-checks, and *The Sufficient Life* (1906), for a loan company.

In many respects the young Peter McArthur typified the farm youth of his and probably every age. As adventure, romantic dreams, the myth of success, or what you will lured them to the city, so, too, was McArthur lured. Yet for him the attraction differed, for he dreamed of fame as a writer and believed that only New York could make it possible. Such thinking was common among budding Canadian authors of the time, and many made it their mecca. Accordingly, in 1890, when McArthur arrived in New York, full of buoyant hopes, he was delighted to make friends with the distinguished poets Charles G. D. Roberts and Bliss Carman, the painter Charles W. Jefferys, and other members of the little colony of Canadian expatriates that had grown up there. In this New York venture, however, there were two McArthurs, one with his heart in the country, and the other with his eyes on Parnassus. McArthur's letters to his New York friend C. B. Vaux reveal the split that developed within him. Like most migrants to the city, he had not only the pressures of urban living to contend with but also those that derived from his country upbringing.

McArthur differed from other expatriates of the time in that he returned to Canada to make his name as a writer, not as novelist or poet, but as a nature writer and, then, not as Rousseauistic dreamer, Thoreauvian transcendentalist, or animal psychologist like Ernest Thompson Seton and Charles G. D. Roberts, but as a farmer describing the thoughts and experiences of his everyday life. Each week from 1909 to 1924, he contributed articles on country life—he called them "country stuff"—to the *Globe*, Toronto, and for almost a decade to the *Farmer's Advocate*. Later he made selections from them for his books *In Pastures Green* (1915) and *The Red Cow* (1919), to rescue his best work from the dust and neglect of newspaper and magazine files and to give impetus to his "back-to-the-land movement." At the time, too, his articles and books had won him such renown and his farmyard animals had gained such "notoriety" that he turned public lecturer for a few months during 1916–1917 to take advantage of his success.

McArthur was not interested basically in entertaining his readers or listeners with accounts of the escapades of the Red Cow or other protagonists of his rural drama, nor in informing them about farm affairs. He wished to preach a way of life. In his youth he had yearned for the culture of the city. Now, in place of "escapism," he proclaimed the cultural value of the simple life. In it nature replaced the arts and was a source of even higher inspiration and greater pleasure. Moreover, since in pioneer communities the arts were normally associated with women, McArthur sought a culture more relevant to the "manly" tradition of the farm world. His cultural heroes were not painters, musicians, or even poets, but the sturdy men of action who had settled the land. Yet here, for all the damning of the city and praise of the country, McArthur seems again a divided soul.

The theme of return runs through much of his writing. It is central in the sonnets, where he prays to return to the good life, and in his "country stuff," where he celebrates the joy of returning home in 1908 to the peace and security of the country and the innocence and memories of his youth, to a world where one was judged not as an artist but as a man of the soil, not by the sophisticated but by the natural and ingenuous. Still, this "return" never removed his deep desire to make his mark as a novelist and poet, an ambition scarcely compatible with the demands of farming. Sometimes he tried to hide it by belittling his own writing or literature in general, or by concealing it behind a façade of humor. For all that, however, he never stopped writing and he never ceased to quote from great writers to make his essays more literary. It is possible, too, that some of his distaste for the city came from envy; although he villified the businessman he never gave up hopes of becoming one himself.

Thomas Hardy said that one must have lived in only one place in order to write well; yet the comment does not apply to McArthur. His sally into urban life preserved him from parochialism. It gave his writing tension and depth. It was the work of farmer-artist-businessman McArthur, of a humanist seriously concerned with setting out a philosophy of life.

There is a danger in pursuing this interpretation of McArthur as divided soul too far, of assuming that the McArthur who took charge of the Liberal election campaign in 1908 was out of character with the writer, or of assuming the same for the McArthur who wrote reams on the revision of the Bank Act, who became provisional director of the Ontario Equitable Trust Corporation (1922) and a spokesman for big life insurance companies, and who proposed a scheme to Henry Ford to help him make money (which the latter turned down and so had to get along making millions in his own old way). Even on his deathbed McArthur dictated an essay on a plan for a spring-water bottling plant for his farm. It is easy to forget here that McArthur lived before the age of specialization and in a new and sparsely populated country where the depersonalizing forces of the modern age had yet to make their full impact. In his day the pioneer concept of the man of parts, the informed amateur, maintained much of its former hold.

The work of McArthur's last few years illustrates the point. *Sir Wilfrid Laurier* was commissioned by one publishing house because of both his friendship with the "Old Chief" and his work for the Liberal party, and *The Affable Stranger* (1920) by another, because of McArthur's interest in both economic and cultural Canadian–United States relationships. Again, there is his *Stephen Leacock* (1923), which he wrote at the request of the Ryerson Press and which has remained one of the best critical studies of McArthur's fellow humorist. More important in terms of this discussion are the pamphlets, especially *The Last Law–Brotherhood* (1921), that McArthur wrote for a large insurance company. At first sight they appear as another indication of McArthur's abiding concern with the business world. Yet they are more than an illustration of that love-hate relationship. They were statements of his belief that life insurance could be the open sesame to a rural utopia. They were in fact McArthur's final attempts to reconcile the conflict between ruralism and urbanism that had troubled him so much and that had marked the transition from the pioneer to the modern. In them he was trying to promote an enterprise that he thought could save the farming community from complete engulfment in a new way of life.

CHAPTER 1

Poet

I Glimpse of Parnassus

IN childhood McArthur developed a love of poetry that was never to leave him. He recalled that as a boy he spent hours listening to tales of Scotland that his parents told until his mind was filled with dreams of events and scenes of the glens and Highlands of Scotland. His essays and poems hint, too, that his father's daily reading of the Bible left a lasting mark. That other Scottish "Bible," the poetry of Robert Burns, seems likewise to have had its effect. At least when a lad, McArthur spent a gift of fifty cents on a volume of Burns rather than on powder and shot, the usual purchase of the country youth of his time. Soon his interests broadened, and Byron and Shelley became favorites. This predilection disturbed his parents, but the poets and young McArthur won the day.

Although McArthur preferred the Romantics and Shakespeare, he read widely not only in British and American literature but also in Canadian. As a young man in Toronto, he had, he said, thrilled to the work of the poets then making their names— Wilfred Campbell, Bliss Carman, Duncan Campbell Scott, Charles G. D. Roberts, and Archibald Lampman. In those days, he says, "a new poem by one of these poets was an event of the first importance. The one who had discovered the poem hurriedly called a conclave in a boarding house ... and we revelled in our find. Our best reader would read it aloud and we would go over it line by line. Those poems meant more to us than 'the glory that was Greece and the grandeur that was Rome.' Our souls vibrated to their new and native melody, and we were proud that the singers were Canadian."[1] McArthur always kept abreast of work of Canadian poets, for he could "never pass a poem without glancing through it."[2] He did not

thrill as when the earlier poets were making their reputations—
"No ardent lights illume the brow / As in the days of old"—but
he did like several of the newer Canadian writers of the early
twentieth century and knew the work of Robert Norwood,
Arthur Phelps, and Arthur Bourinot well. Although basically
conservative in taste, he had no problem later in life, either, in
enjoying poets, especially Whitman, whose mode differed from
that of the Confederation group.

Although in the everyday world the poets were with McArthur
at all times and "their glowing phrases sprang to [his] lips at
every turn," he was left "at the heart of things . . . to stammer for
himself."[3] Even if left to stammer, he never wavered in his
desire to speak the language of poetry. According to his essay
"My Friends, the Trees," he began his stammering early, for in
it he refers to an oak that had enjoyed a joke on him when under
it he had composed a poem that glowed with this gem:

> It long has been my cherished hope
>   Upon my dying day
> To lie down on some sunny slope
>   And dream my life away.

All other stanzas are lost, but the older McArthur's only regret
was that even one line remained. "The old tree," he remarked long
after, "must have chuckled to its last twig at my absurdity.
Anyway," he continues, "I never see the tree without recalling
that wretched stanza, and I immediately hurry away to some
other part of the woods."[4] This stanza is probably all that
remains of the juvenilia that the young McArthur burned in
1885, convinced of his failure as poet. The ceremonial fire was
scarcely ashes, however, before a rejuvenated bard was submitting fresh efforts to the bright new Toronto magazine, *Saturday Night;* and so it went. The struggle for the peak of Parnassus
was never ending, however intermittent, and in his last year he
was "writing poetry with the abandon of a school boy," which
he intended editing "into such a poem as [he had] always wanted
to write."[5]

Among the many romantic poets whom McArthur admired
only Roberts, whose sonnets he ranked with the greatest, and

Whitman, whose work attracted him in his later years, seem to have influenced his style of poetry. He loved to quote his old friend Carman, and not merely the "charming and exquisite Carman" of Rufus Hathaway's edition of his work, *Bliss Carman's Poems* (1929), but he seldom tried to imitate Carman's kind of verse. Carman, however, did much to strengthen the romantic element in McArthur's attitude to art and life. He taught McArthur that "it is only after facts have dissolved and vanished into the mystery of things that the poetic soul can begin to recreate, and devise forms of beauty."[6] Under Carman's influence, McArthur came more and more to accept the anti-intellectualism and the nature worship that characterize much romantic poetry. "It was not through knowledge that the poets reached their sublimities, but through feeling," he exclaims, calling on Keats, Wordsworth, and Shakespeare to support his argument and on Carman's "Let me taste the old immortal / Indolence of life once more" to clinch it. From this poem, if fully realized, he contended, you can get more than "from all the books and all the colleges," for it "puts us in harmony with the universe."[7]

Life at Amityville, Long Island, with Jay Hambidge also helped reinforce McArthur's idealism. The two men were working on a theory of art that Hambidge called dynamic symmetry, the aesthetic that grew out of their studies of Greek architecture and sculpture and that attempted to formulate a natural law of proportion based on a definite mathematical ratio between area measurements of the human body. As Hambidge put it, this ratio, or "theme," differs for almost every individual. "Every human being has within himself—apart from his mind or soul— something of the godlike and this something is the character perfection contained in his symmetry."[8] Here was music to McArthur's ears. The new philosophy verified a natural law of beauty and of another of the main tenets of romantic aesthetics, the dignity of the individual. In the long run, he was to find Hambidge's theory unacceptable, for it stressed the mathematical and rational at the expense of the intuitional and emotional. The stanza composed under the oak contained more truth than poetry, but it contained truth. For the time, however, McArthur had no doubts about the purport of dynamic symmetry.

As a result of this fresh enthusiasm, McArthur seems to have been confused about the aims of poetry. At one extreme, he considered it a means of stirring appreciation of the grandeur of nature, that feeling, that longing for infinity, he experienced when he gazed over his beloved countryside at Ekfrid. Nature was superior to poetry, but inspired poetry. It follows, then, that in accordance with Carman's philosophy, the greatest "art" of all was participation in nature, "to give oneself to a reverie that can never be formulated in words ... in which one apprehends beauties that no poet can express." "After all," McArthur asks, "do the poets amount to so very much?" And he replies, "Out in the woods I do not feel they do."[9] This is McArthur at his most perverse, or his most enthusiastically romantic. In general here, however, he sees the artist as one who helps cleanse the doors of perception in order to put man "in accord with the great rhythms of the universe ... [when] poetry becomes as natural as breathing."[10]

At the other extreme, McArthur preached that the aim of poetry was not to induce dreams, but to waken the reader to living the good life. Since the dynamic—growth or motion from the whorl of leaves to the movement of the planets—was the basis of the new aesthetic, action, always considered by the idealist a function in developing self, likewise took on new meaning. McArthur saw now that deeds were superior to dreams: "Deeds are the right and only alphabet / Wherewith to teach what all the world should know."[11]

Both extremes reduce the poet to silence, but according to McArthur's Amityville philosophy the greatest art is the good life. Words, if words at all, were to serve as guides, to perform a social function, and literature became largely a matter of propaganda. McArthur had learned years before that the word had meaning as it related to man's spirituality and his God. Although he had had a heavy diet of Gaelic Bible as a child, it had been prescribed for his moral, not his aesthetic, benefit. That he wrote poems in the name of a philosophy that stressed moral action is not so paradoxical as it first appears. They simply argued for it. Much of their high seriousness assuredly derives, also, from the fact that McArthur was living through a troubled period, licking his wounds after the loss of his position as editor of *Truth* and the enervating Bohemianism of his first years in New

York. In this sense many of his sonnets were self-admonitory
soliloquies and prayers for spiritual strength.

McArthur's case for deed disturbed William Deacon, his
official biographer, for he thought it flawed McArthur's philosophy
of life, which, McArthur being a poet, he considered would center in the intellect and the imagination. In this assessment, Deacon
only touches on the influence of McArthur's religious background,
and ignores entirely the impact on McArthur of the frontier,
where the man of action was the "hero." As a result Deacon
looks on McArthur's theme in the sonnets as aberration largely,
rather than as revelation of a deeply ingrained attitude. On
another level he fails to note McArthur's distrust of words that
stems from his newspaper work and his awareness of the way in
which they can become tools for deceit and special pleading.
Yet admitting the incongruity of a writer preaching action as
the only valid response to life, one can reconcile the "poetic"
or imaginative response to it that McArthur recommends in the
nature poems in *The Prodigal* and the active response he demands
in those that are religious-philosophical. In the one, action
means deeds done in accordance with the values of "Amityville
idealism" and, in the other, it means dreaming, for through it
one can enter "the heavens the poets have given." Action and
dreams were, then, two sides of the same coin. Poetry that produced good deeds or induced reverie taught that the ideal is the
real and led to action in either the actual or the intuitional world.
Escapist poetry was an escape into life, not from it, but whether
reveries or deeds were superior to art, McArthur never wavered
in his belief that poetry could produce both.

II   The Prodigal and Other Poems

McArthur published at least 185 poems, but only three books
of poetry. All appeared early in his career and all are thin
volumes containing all told forty-two different poems—*Five
Sonnets* (1899), *Lines* (1901), and *The Prodigal and Other
Poems* (1907). Of all these poems, twenty-four are sonnets,
mostly of the Shakespearean form, although one, "The True
Evangel," with only four rhyming words, surpasses even the
petrarchan pattern for tightness of ryhme. The first fifteen son-

nets in *The Prodigal,* which had already appeared in *Lines,* formed a sequence designed as "landmarks of my struggling soul / That moves through doubt to its victorious goal,"[12] or a return to innocence. To enjoy life, as he put it later, you must "loaf and invite the boy in you."[13] As a joyous father welcomes the return of his son in "The Prodigal," so the older McArthur welcomes back his own youth:

> And I, the slave of patience, took him in,
>   Gave him my heart and bade him welcome home,
> Thrilled with his dreams of all I yet may win—
>   Allured again in golden paths to roam,
> And now I know life has no greater joy
> Than, having lived, to be once more a boy.[14]

Likewise, God welcomes back the repentant soul, the soul that, though "long lost," started with "pure, resplendent raptures" of youth. "So we, through God... / Nor grope in darkness nor in weakness fall."[15]

The sonnet sequence never makes clear where McArthur found God, but "Dear Mother Nature" of the sonnet "Earthborn" at least shares His presence; she is the source of his dreams and the refuge of his soul:

> Dear Mother Nature, not in vain we ask
> Of thee for strength! The visioned victories
> Revive my heart, and golden honors gleam:
> For here, once more, while in thy love I bask,
> My soul puts forth her rapid argosies
> To the uncharted ports of summer dream.[16]

Yet the sonnets, which like fingerposts mark the spiritual route the prodigal traveled, might well have pointed the way for Bunyan's Christian. Here is "Aspiration"; here, "Duty" and "Reticence" leading a little farther on to "Consecration" and, finally, via "Solace," "De Profundis," and "Courage," to "Summum Bonum."

Serious and solemn, the sequence follows fairly closely the Old Testament teaching about faith and life lived according to God's will. "And then will deeds with love and patience fraught / Through God to man reveal life's high emprise."[17] And

then, too, "The freedom of the infinite is mine."[18] There seems
some whistling in the dark here and there, but the poems conclude with hopes that heaven will be the reward of everyone,
repentant sinners and all, who have accepted and lived according to the covenant of works.

> But they that in the market-place we meet,
> Each with his trumpet and his noisy faction,
> Are leaky vessels, pouring on the street
> The truth they know ere it hath known its action.
> Yet which think ye, in His benign regard,
> Or words or deeds shall merit the reward?[19]

All the sonnets in *The Prodigal,* even those outside the Prodigal
sequence, are philosophical and didactic with the exception of an
elegy to D. A. McKellar and "The Ocean Liner." Some celebrate
"warriors lean" in "The Shaw Memorial," and others, the great
artists Sarah Bernhardt and Shakespeare. Some discuss idealism,
and others, natural religion, and, in "The Salt Marshes," McArthur
tries to make a case for "the rhythmus of immortal deeds" as
part of the universal principle of motion. McArthur prized these
poems highly and thought them philosophically challenging—and
they sometimes are challenging but seldom philosophically. They
are difficult, if difficult, not because of the obscurity of profundity but because of the obscurity of complexity. They can be
paradoxical and even metaphysical. Their rhyme schemes often
give rise to strangely involuted lines, and McArthur's need to
condense frequently results in inadequately expressed ideas,
although he shows considerable technical skill in handling
the sonnet.

For the most part McArthur's sonnets are too abstract, a flaw
that a host of personified abstractions does not remedy. They are
poems of statement, not metaphor, and generally, also, when
metaphorical, they rely on established and, hence, trite imagery.
Occasionally they do take on impressive imaginative overtones,
however, to rise above a level of high competency. The poet
reveres the country where, he feels, his "soul puts forth her
rapid argosies / To the uncharted ports of summer dream." Or
impressed with the modernity of an ocean liner, he presents her
in a strong imagist poem:

Like some bewildered monster of the deep,
Groping to freedom through the baffling tide,
   She blunders forth, while nuzzling at her side
The blustering harbor craft about her creep.
Anon she feels her iron pulses leap,
   And, symbol of the age's mastering pride,
   Looks out to where the ocean stretches wide,
Scorning the fears that in its mystery sleep.
All day with headlong and undoubting haste,
   And all the night upon her path she flames
      Like some weird shape from olden errantry;
And when some wafted wanderer of the waste
   A storm-worn pennant dips afar, proclaims
      With raucous voice her strong supremacy.[20]

The Prodigal contains other "serious" poetry, but McArthur
has descended from the "heights" in it. Nature, not the soul,
becomes his subject, but pastoral nature, not the divine nature of
the romantic dreamers. Anthologists have found this kind of
poetry McArthur's most attractive. Whereas only two sonnets
have achieved the permanence of a place in two of the standard
Canadian collections, five other poems from *The Prodigal*—
"Corn Planting," "Sugar Weather," "An Indian Love Song,"
"The End of the Drought," and "To the Birds"—have appeared
in a half dozen Canadian anthologies of poetry. Most include
only one or two, but John Garvin's important collection *Canadian
Poets* (1916) contains the five mentioned.

Of all these poems a stanza from "Sugar Weather," which
poem has proven the most popular, well exemplifies this kind of
McArthur's nature poetry.

When snow-balls pack on the horses' hoofs
   And the wind from the south blows warm,
When the cattle stand where the sunbeams beat
   And the noon has a dreamy charm,
When icicles crash from the dripping eaves
   And the furrows peep black through the snow,
Then I hurry away to the sugar bush,
   For the sap will run, I know.[21]

Realistically descriptive, with a wash of sentiment, this sort of
verse appealed to the critics of the early decades of the century,

as a change in diet from Carman's escapism and Roberts's meta-physics. Here was a Canadian poem about "real" Canadian life. Vividly detailed, it yet carried overtones of something beyond the present and the parochial, and seemed a proof of the poetic merits of the homespun.

III   They Shall Inherit the Earth

After *The Prodigal*, McArthur wrote serious poetry only oc-casionally, but with a difference. Only twice did he return to Car-man's dreamland nature, where, as the sonnet "Fulfillment," which concludes *Friendly Acres*, proclaims "in the fields the troubled vision clears," and where, according to "A Defence," he would lie in the sun and fill his "soul till [he] did not care, / Though barns were empty and fields were bare."[22] He had begun, how-ever, to discover this kind of poetry inadequate for what he wanted to say. Living on the Ekfrid farm differed from living there in memory. Moreover, that farm world for which the romantic and lyrical were suited seemed to be slipping away, eroded by modernity and materialism. It needed a poetry to restate its values and celebrate its people.

McArthur's bucolic poetry differed, then, from his early verse of the kind, such as "A Farm Song," "Corn Planting," and "Sugar Weather." They were idylls; those written at Ekfrid were not. They belong to the literature of protest. McArthur had, in fact, barely returned there before he published "The Farmer's Satur-day Night," which, though cut from Burns's cloth, centers on a grumbling farmer who has become a victim of urban forces. Before long McArthur had, also, thrown down a challenge to the world of bright lights with "A Farmer's Defence," which forms the conclusion of *In Pastures Green*, and warns that without the farmer "your wonder world / Would hungry go and bare"; and with "The Burden of Labour," a new sort of lyric with these lines as refrain:

> Thy little birds a-lilting
>   Come back to us each spring,
> But we who feed the nations,
>   We are too tired to sing.[23]

Paralleling this poetry of social criticism was his poetry of affirmation, in which McArthur sang the praises of the pioneers, from whom the farmers, he had insisted, inherited their place as true nation builders. He had begun his crusade for a greater appreciation of Canadian tradition with "The Pioneers," on the men who "wrought like heroes in their Promised Land," and concluded it in the year of his death with "The Home Dream." Half autobiography and half history, this is a long, stanzaic poem designed to foster his "back-to-the-land movement" and to sum up his tributes over the years to those who had lived by "The old dream, the home dream, / The little dream come true."[24] Poems of social purpose, these are largely significant as illustrations of the growth of McArthur's social consciousness, for, in a development that runs counter to the normal, he became more "radical" with age. The poetry of his youth had been largely concerned with the individual (whatever the relational role with society, God, or nature), that of his later years with man as a class and with nature, but only rarely, and as social determinant. This social awareness derived from his romantic idealism, for it centered in respect for values of the past and admiration of the people of the time for their struggles, not for survival, but for self-fulfillment.

Convinced of the spiritual greatness of the pioneers and of the supremacy of the natural over the sophisticated, McArthur sought a poetry that expressed these ideas in appropriate form. He wanted a poet who could sing democracy in the voice of the people and celebrate the egalitarianism that he associated with frontier life. This poet he found in Whitman, who despite his stress on individualism made mankind his subject and who confirmed romantic idealism by revealing the place of "Cosmic consciousness"[25] in everyday life. Besides, he "was not an artist like Shakespeare and did not try to devise art forms in which to give his soul expression. He simply reported what he saw and realized, in a form and language that seemed to him the most natural and expressive."[26] Under the persuasion of such thinking McArthur made Whitman his model for his most ambitious later poems, "The Stone," "A Chant of War," "A Chant of Mammonism," and "The Unknown Soldier," which remains a great unruly mass of some hundred or so manuscript pages, a

challenge to any who would try to organize it, but yet moving
and convincing evidence of McArthur's lifelong dedication to
poetry.[27]

Although these four are poems of social criticism, they focus
on different areas of concern. "The Stone," written in 1912, is an
allegory of a poor man who dug out of a road a stone that
people, because of their lack of public spirit, had never once
tried to remove, though they had bumped over it for three
generations. The poor man had simply done a humble task, "not
waiting for an order," and had put society to shame, for the
stone was discovered to be "about the size of a milk pail." With
this event as support, the poet concludes with a shout, "Tremble,
ye Oppressors! Quake, ye Financial Pirates!" for "there is a man
loose in Canada" who "makes smooth the way of the Worker."
"The Chant of War," written not long after McArthur's abortive
"talking picture"[28] of Whitman's war poems, marked the beginning of what was to be "the epic of the new world." John Smith,
its hero, again the common man, in this poem removes no stone,
but fights nobly, determined not to stop until he has "destroyed
war."

Like "The Stone" and "A Chant of War," "A Chant of Mammonism" bears many marks of Whitman's influence—catalogues
of events, repetitions of words and ideas, varying line lengths,
and similar prosodic characteristics. For all its merits, however,
it, like the other poems, illustrates the difficulty of directly
imitating greatness. "A Chant of Mammonism" deserves attention
as much for its introduction and recent comments on it as it does
for its content. The poet addresses himself in his preface to his
new theory of art and economics. In the first he declares that
since he is "convinced the critic of the future will find most
important contributions to the literature of our time in the
advertisements that announce and commend our commercial and
industrial adventures ... [he had] written what is frankly an
advertisement." As regards the second theory, he proclaims life
insurance "the Democracy of finance." Despite the directness of
McArthur's statements here, however, modern criticism has tried
to sum up all McArthur's social theories under the agrarian myth.
The passages from which the quotations are taken, says F. W.
Watt, "suggest the enthusiasm with which he threw himself, at

that time in his career, into the life of modern commercial civilization." But, he continues, "In 1908 . . . McArthur abandoned his commercial and literary adventures" and returned to Ekfrid.[29] This is a complete misunderstanding of McArthur, for he wrote the poem in 1922 (and not before 1908) and when he had come to believe that insurance presented the one way of reconciling ruralism and big business.

IV *Cap and Bells*

The best poetry in *The Prodigal* is its excellent light verse. Spiced with satire or leavened with good-natured humor, it acts as a countermeasure to the sobersided poems. McArthur pokes fun at the moderns—Tolstoi, Ibsen, Schopenhauer, and Howells. He berates the birds for their merry songs and bids them model themselves on the famous of the time:

> All happiness they sadly shirk,
>   And from all pleasure hold aloof,
> And are so tearful when they work
>   They write on paper waterproof,
> And on each express a yearn
> To fill a cinerary urn.[30]

Bad literary criticism this may be, but the satire rises to humor, thanks to the clever diction and imagery. Or consider the plight of parents whose child attends an up-to-date school:

> They teach him physiology,
>   And, O, it chills our hearts
> To hear our prattling innocent
>   Mix up his inward parts.[31]

Occasionally McArthur makes a volte-face as in this anti-Arcadian *vers de société* (once a popular form with him), "To My Fashionable Fiancée":

> And I'd not care to gather haws
>   And sit in thorny shades to chew them,
> And who would pipe on oaten straws
>   When he might suck mint-juleps through them!

In sooth, we're better as we are:
    Your gravest task to baffle freckles,
And mine to keep all care afar
    And work for the elusive shekels.[32]

Though light, "In Oblivion," one of McArthur's several dramatic
monologues, is more impressive than any of the other poems
on the eternal virtues. It presents its point about life with a
restraint and urbanity that make even more ironical its theme
of the irony of life, which Death the leveler holds forever his.
To begin, the poet proposes "a merry meeting / After the play,"
where "Our masks we'll throw aside" and to conclude tries, with
this piece of metaphysics, to persuade his friend to attend:

Methinks that there, my friend, both you and I
    Can fleet away eternity content;
No curious fool into our lives can pry
    And moralize on how our days are spent;
And soon, how soon! the names that flare on high
    Will wane and with the closing night be blent;
For while we revel in Oblivion
The great must join us one by one.[33]

After *The Prodigal* McArthur persisted with his light verse,
and developed a parody ballade as a weapon for satire. He
wrote at least nine—of Bugs, Cows, Apples, Unanswered Letters, and other similar prosaic subjects. They are ephemera,
but they are good fun with their clever lines and sometimes out-
rageous rhymes. If the poet fails to follow the French form he
excuses himself on the basis of "many precedents for variations"
and, to add to their mockery, he addresses almost all to the
Prince of Wales.

McArthur's satire often lost its edge, however, dulled by a
reiteration of attacks on politicians and financiers, as in his series
of satiric limericks on Sir Jingo McBore, the composite personi-
fication of both *bêtes noires*. Once, though, McArthur, in his
"serious" light verse, fused social comment and satire on a level
above the merely critical and the blunt when he took Tutankhamen as subject. He began by asking direct and ironically
irreverent questions:

Tutankhamen, aroused from spicy slumbers,
What think you of our methods up-to-date?
(I scarce know how to weave your name in numbers—
Should I stress ante- or penultimate?)

He draws his questions to a close with further questions that
imply what McArthur's, if not King Tutankhamen's, answers are:

What would we think if to Westminster Abbey
    Some ghoul should come on an ill-fated day
And in the name of Science hire a cabby
    To cart the bones of Wellington away?

"How are ye blind," so sang the Grecian poet,
    "Who waste the tombs where ancient heroes lie!"
What is this knowledge that we need to know it?
    What is your gain? "Yourselves so soon to die!"[34]

For sheer good humor and high-spirited poetry nothing in
Canadian literature can surpass "A Crane Song" and "The
Mockingbird." The first, a chant in reply to those who questioned
McArthur's observation that cranes can sing, gives those orni-
thological doubting Thomases a disarming answer, frivolous as
he considers the whole dispute to be. The poet is peremptory
with the poor cranes, ordering them about in a pseudoserious
manner, for McArthur intends to call on no muses to win his
case. The cranes alone are to give him victory:

Spear the pop-eyed frog!
Shatter the succulent clam!
But, above all things, dance and sing,
For I am fain to join your stilted saraband!
I feel that your voices are the only ones my voice will chord with.

As an earnest of his comradeship and a celebration of victory,
he promises the cranes a treat in such a way as to turn farce
into humor of character, whereby he raucously derides the
sobersided and teaches them something about enjoying nature
and life in the right spirit.

Wherefore, O cranes and herons, rejoice!
Some day I shall go wading with you,
And perhaps we'll also make a night of it!
"Awk, awk, awk!" Prance high and be happy.[35]

Or consider that other piece of tomfoolery that illustrates Mc-
Arthur's amazing ability to quote bits and pieces from almost
everyone and here to fuse them to make him a literary mockingbird in both senses of the word:

Mock, throw away and recapture again!
"Hark! Hark" the lark at heaven's gate sings,
    And Phoebus 'gins arise,
His steeds to water at the springs
On chaliced flowers that lies.

(Parse it! Parse it! Tweedle-dee-dee!
    Silly grammarian, see! see! see!)[36]

If McArthur's light verse does not belong in the highest class
of poetry, it stands high in the order to which it does belong.
Had it said the same thing in prose, it undoubtedly would have
a recognized place in our literature, for the humorous essay
appears to be a more accepted genre than the humorous poem.
But then Arnold ruled Chaucer out of court because he lacked
"high seriousness."

CHAPTER 2

Author

I *Other Strings to His Bow*

M cARTHUR began writing prose at an early age, when, aspiring to publication in the Toronto *Saturday Night*, he began submitting short stories to his friend Duncan McKellar, then on staff with the magazine. McKellar rejected the stories. At the same time he advised McArthur that the short story is a definite art form with a pattern revolving around a single incident and with several other dependent characteristics. The lesson sank deep apparently, since McArthur's early short stories kept close to the "rules," but he was scarcely at home in the form. In the tale, the moral fable, and the burlesque (which also comprised some of his work in short fiction), on the other hand, he was completely at home. All told, however, he published only thirty pieces belonging to these various genres.

According to Deacon, McArthur thought these early stories were of little merit. "After he got back to [Ekfrid] a dozen or so of these casually begotten productions were returned to him as unfit even for boiler plate. At the same time he got a request from the *Canadian Magazine* for stories, and sent those in. They were all published with illustrations; and in Poole's International Guide to Periodical Literature you find them all listed solemnly under his name. He was much peeved when I put them in my bibliography."[1] McArthur may have been peeved, but either Deacon's or McArthur's account does not fit the facts. These stories were not "casually begotten," and few, if any, were returned to McArthur in Ekfrid as rejected boiler plate. McArthur's diary refutes Deacon. It reads: "March 3 [1895]. Spent the day working on a story called 'With the Aid of the Widow' to try on 'Town Topics.' ... [February] 26. Sent Harper's 'The

Overlooking of Gideon.' "[2] These and other magazines mentioned in the diary were not the kind to which one sent boiler plate stories intentionally. Moreover, fifteen of the stories, allegedly returned as unfit even for boiler plate, had already appeared in print.

"The Daughter of the Horse-Leech" typifies much of McArthur's work in the short story vis-à-vis the tale. It recounts stiffly an incident in which a young woman, the daughter of the "ogre" who forecloses a mortgage on a poor but honest mortgagee, turns against her father and bravely offers herself in marriage to the penniless young man. Aside from a fine *in medias res* beginning with an auction sale, the story has little to commend it, for it is melodramatic and formidably didactic, its fine beginning more than overbalanced by this concluding scene: " 'And you are sure,' she persisted, 'that you will never despise me for throwing myself at you like this' "

"His answer was: 'Who can find a virtuous woman? for her price is far above rubies. The heart of her husband doth safely trust in her, so that he shall have no need to spoil.' "[3] Typical, also, except for the religious overtones, are its use of characters as narrative pegs and its happy ending.

By and large McArthur's short stories proper are gimmicky and often pseudosophisticated. They are contrived and center entirely in incident and the actions of stereotype characters. Frequently the romance (and all McArthur's short stories are about romantic love) is inconsequential to the last degree. Two young people decide to test their tempers in "An Experiment in Wisdom"; a bashful lover falls off his bicycle to win the attention of an angelic young woman and, proposing that "he'll work and be a success when he is away," he wins her in "Riding for a Fall." And so on through a half dozen or more other screeds of romantic comedy.

Of course *Truth* was an open sesame for McArthur and, aside from his short stories, he contributed to it a series more to his liking called "Tales of Millionaires." Freed from the demands of plot, as he understood it, his writing lost much of its stiffness. He could concentrate on character without trying to fit it into a pattern of events and, no longer restricted by the demands of the conventional love story, he could more fully turn his natural bent for satire and humor to profitable account. In fact, in this series of five tales he took the opportunity to reveal the flaws of the big capitalists—their failure to appreciate the "finer things of life" and their loneliness as the result of their worship of money—as he could scarcely have revealed them in the editorial page of the magazine. Still, the wealthy hero in "A Good Time Coming" stepped on few capitalists' toes when he decided not to donate money to help support a poverty-stricken friend since it would destroy his initiative and remove his reasons for hope. One of these tales, "Art in Money Making," is little more than an argument between a writer and a businessman that derides the typical American self-made man who is secretly proud that he "never had a chance to learn" the sophisticated way of life, and who boasts, "I made my own fortune, didn't inherit it, and am and always will be a rough and ready chap." The story of the writer who has made a million dollars as a businessman is obviously wish-fulfillment, McArthur's lifelong dream. In addition he discusses a theory of art similar to McArthur's in that it holds experience the only source of material for writing and the romantic the only valid perspective.

Of the five tales, "The Genial Mr. Peabody," actually a moral fable, is by far the best. A newspaperman, a central character in many of McArthur's short pieces, visits a retired, wealthy businessman who prides himself on his humor, and whom his servants pretend to find hilariously funny. The story lightly satirizes almost everything it touches without once becoming cynical—newsmen, the yellow press, mystery stories, servants, and masters. It has just enough of the ridiculous to lift it out of the matter-of-fact into an amusing and make-believe world, where satire seems merely a part of the romantic view.

Since the humor permeates the whole account, one may nibble anywhere to get its flavor, but the conclusion in particular demonstrates McArthur's talent for depicting humorous character and scene. Mr. Peabody tells one of his jokes to his servants and the "hero," Percy Duval, to his great dismay, finds that the following has been the cause of a mysterious burst of laughter he had just heard.

"O, I was just telling them" says Mr. Peabody, "that whenever
I go to New York I go to pieces . . . . to see pieces at the theatre,
you know."

Again the inextinguishable laughter of the servants broke out,
each trying to surpass the others, and as Percy looked from Mr.
Peabody to them and back again, the humor of the situation over-
came him so that he laughed as he had not laughed for years. . . .
From that time Percy Duval's downfall began. . . . [Mr. Peabody]
was so delighted at finding that his wit was appreciated by a bright
New York newspaper man, that he would dodge out from behind
a clump of shrubbery and say to him after leading him aside from
the rest of the family: . . . .

"Why does Bryan's name suggest that he will be defeated in the
election?"

Percy would give up.

"Bryan, Bry n, brine, Salt Creek. He'll go up Salt Creek. See?"
and the old man would punch him in the ribs with a pudgy fat fist
till Percy would grunt with discomfort and grin in despair. So it
was day after day. Mr. Peabody persisted in getting off puns that
only a millionaire from whom one had great expectations or a great
employer of labor can be allowed to perpetrate and yet live. At last
the strain became too great for [Percy] and he hurried back to Park
Row and took to drink.[4]

"The Genial Mr. Peabody," along with "A Moral Bully"
(1897) and three pieces published in *Ourselves* during 1910,
"My Neighbor the Corporation," "Jim Cook's Vote," and "The
Row in the North Riding," surpass all other fiction McArthur
ever wrote. (The first three are moral fables and the others,
burlesques.) In his other stories and tales the characters were
largely plot-ridden and the humor, normally stilted comedy
of incident, sometimes a violent and crude slapstick. Moreover,
they were almost always concerned with the sophisticated and
urban, in which McArthur was seldom comfortable. In his
best fiction, character is central, and the humor—and all his
best fiction is humorous—is usually satirical, thus giving a
depth and purport lacking in his other stories, even serious
ones such as "The Transfiguration of Jameson," in which a
millionaire finally learns to love his family above his money.
In addition almost all his best fiction has a setting that could

easily be part of the Little Town that Leacock described in his *Sunshine Sketches of a Little Town*.

Aside from the humor, to be discussed in another chapter, the stories alluded to have many other excellencies. Each centers in a single event: "A Moral Bully" in Mr. Silas Bostick's visit to Mr. Jonas Slambang to forgive him for permitting his horse to get into Mr. Bostick's garden, where it trampled the flowers; "My Neighbor the Corporation" in the establishing of the Cackling Hen Merger in a village; "Jim Cook's Vote" and "The Row in the North Riding" in the attempts of political parties to secure the noncommitted vote of dim-witted Jim Cook, who lacked "the great political virtue of staying bought," and, in the second story, in the Liberals' efforts to settle a squabble over the appointment of a postmaster for Siasconsette.

Although each story revolves around a single incident, the incident is important only as the generating circumstance of a conflict that develops themes by revealing character—Mr. Bostick as a man of exasperating and Uriah Heepish goodness; the little man as victim of the depersonalizing forces of big business; politicians as unprincipled and voters as gullible.

McArthur is especially good at introducing his themes with opening sentences that both hint at coming events and suggest their orientations, such as this from "Jim Cook's Vote": "Though all votes are equally sacred, all votes are not equally important"; or this from "My Neighbor the Corporation": "When the Cackling Hen Merger was formed I had more cause than most men to be interested." The conclusions bring these stories full circle, but are old-fashioned in that they sum up the meaning of the story. Indeed, "My Neighbor the Corporation" drops the guise of fiction to become a commentary on the malpractices of the financial world.

McArthur often develops his theme by dramatizing it in dialogue that is natural to the character and is also functional in disclosing his personality and in moving the narrative along.

Here is a line or two of Mr. and Mrs. Brown's conversation when Mrs. Brown knows what her husband does not even suspect—that he had been hoodwinked by political flattery:

When she had read the newspaper she simply said:
   "Well?"

"Did you notice, mother, that they speak of me as a leading Liberal?"

"Huh," she snorted, "When you were doing your leading I didn't notice that you led yourself into the postmastership."

"But my dear, you don't understand—"

"Oh, don't I, though. I understand that we are still in the grocery business when we had been expecting for ten years to settle down in our old age in the post office. If you have anything more to do with the 'Liberal Party' you are an old fool, and that's all I've got to say about it."[5]

When McArthur wishes, he can also describe character so as to fit it into narrative and theme without turning it into a fictional robot, as witness Mr. Henry Allen, who has just learned that he is a "leading Liberal" in an editorial in *Whoop*.

Allen read to the end of the editorial, but the convincing peroration was lost on him. On every line he could see "Leading Liberal, Henry Allen." As a matter of fact he had never led anything more important than a halter broke cow in his life, but he was the most prominent member of a large relationship of Allens, and as they all went together on public questions he came to be regarded as leader, though in reality he was more often pushed than leading. In spite of all this, the phrase "leading Liberal" sounded good to him. After he had handed back the paper to the boy, who promptly rushed to the house to show it to his mother, he went on feeding the squealing pigs. Under cover of the noise, as he was stooping to get out another pailful, he whispered "leading Liberal" into the swill-barrel. When he went to milk the cows the phrase was sounding in his head like a big drum at the Orange celebration. "Leading Liberal," he whispered to himself as he pushed against the ribs of the Jersey, and she, being a cow with a sense of humor, promptly kicked over the pail. At the supper table he was silent and aloof, and when the dishes had been cleared away he got down his razor and shaving mug, so that while shaving he could see just what a "leading Liberal" looked like in the cracked mirror. Then he put on his Sunday clothes and drove up the village. As the horses' hoofs clattered along the gravel road they fitted to a little tune that was running in his head:
"Leading Liberal, leading Liberal,
Hen-ry Allen, leading Liberal."[6]

For *Ourselves,* McArthur wrote much short fiction based on history, his reborn interest in pioneer life almost dictating the subject. He had begun it with "The Over-looking of Gideon" in 1895, but had dropped it for sixteen years, when he took it up again in "Pushing the Sun."[7] Both tales are historical fiction, dramatizing events in the life of William "Tiger" Dunlop that stress his idiosyncrasies. In the first tale he is more than matched by "stout Gideon" McPherson, who believes he has been overlooked by the Evil Eye. Tiger diagnoses the ailment as ague and cures the fortunate Gideon with whiskey so effectively that before the day is out he has become well enough to vanquish a drunken Irishman in an enjoyable brawl that concludes the reaping bee. The story as art is of little account though its atmosphere and tone are consistent and appropriate. Besides, the realism of some parts and especially of this vignette is impressive, so much so that C. W. Jefferys chose it as the subject of one of his three illustrations of the story in the *Canadian Magazine*.

"Ah was takin' rail teemer oot o' ta swamp when ah felt ta tribble; but ahm theenkin' ah may hae been ower-looked when ah was veesitin' in York at the New Year," Gideon explained.

"Umph," said the "Tiger." "Pit oot yer tongue."

Gideon protruded for his scrutiny a tongue like a razor strop.

"That will do. Let me try yer pulse. Umph. Yer in a bad way. . . ."

[Ascertaining the cause], "Tiger" prescribed mighty potations. . . . "Drink, mon," he would say. "Ye are no lang for this warl at the best, so droon yer sorrow. Ye ken what Solomon says on that heid, an' wha are ye to question his weesdom. 'Gi strong drink unto him that is ready to perish.' An' it wull preserve yer corp, mon. Shakspeer says 'a tanner wull last ye nine year,' but I swear a mon beeried wi' a skinfu' o' Canada fusky wull last auchteen."

Gideon shook his head feebly but obeyed the instructions of his physician and long before noon his soul was stirring within him mightily.[8]

In "Pushing the Sun," Tiger is more than matched by his crony Colonel Talbot, who tricks Tiger into bringing out his liquor cabinet, "the thirteen apostles," before noon, that divine moment when he felt morally free to begin drinking.

Although an anecdote, the tale indicates by comparison with "The Over-looking of Gideon" and several short pieces written at the time for *Ourselves* and the *Farmer's Advocate* to what extent McArthur had come to accept the historical, often blended with the emotional, as a substitute for the imaginative, in the short story. The other short pieces referred to, "The Wilderness," "Raising a Log Barn," and so on, are accounts of the settlement of Ontario by a fictitious pioneer. Except for the narrator, however, the stories scarcely belong with fiction, since they are little more than early social history masquerading under fictional guise.

The pioneer seems to belong with Neil McAlpine, who, according to "Bushel for Bushel," saved the Talbot settlement from starvation, and with that other venerable Scot, Baldy McSporran, who seems to have something legendary about him, too, as the result of his will bequeathing orders for coffins and tombstones to his relatives, since he knew "they would put his money in the bank, and . . . that all they would get from it would be good coffins and pleasant tombstones."[9] These character sketches were the last short pieces in which fiction at least flickered. McArthur tried to work on a larger canvas for many more years, but by 1912 his days as a writer of short stories, moral fables, and semifictional tales had in truth come to an end.

Ever resourceful, McArthur later turned to the beast fable as a form suited to goading the urban world. As a youth he had liked George T. Lanigan's *Fables of George Washington Aesop* (1878), which made fables of the news of the day in New York, and, during McArthur's editorship, *Truth* had used the same kind of fable to satirize contemporary society. Similarly, following World War I, disillusioned by the materialism and the bickering over peace in the brave new world, McArthur found it a short, sharp weapon to attack those he assumed were responsible for the national malaise and one that he could smuggle past unsympathetic editors, and from late 1918 to early 1920 published no fewer than twenty-six "Farm Fables" in the *Globe.*

Most of these centered in the traditional animals of the genre —foxes, hares, tortoises, sheep, wolves, and dogs. The fables were traditional also in tone and attitude in allegories like this:

Once upon a time, in a fat agricultural district, the farmers and shepherds were much troubled by having their sheep killed and worried. It was suspected that the damage was the work of wolves, and the watchdogs did a lot of barking about the matter, because it raised the cost of living.

From time to time committees of watchdogs were appointed to investigate the situation, but they always brought in reports that the wolves of the district were nice, quiet wolves, that never did anything that a self-respecting wolf need not be expected to do in the course of his business.

And the depredations of the flocks continued.

Moral: It is not a bad idea to examine the mouths of the watchdogs once in a while to see if they have wool on their teeth.[10]

The traditional animals did not always have leading roles in these fables. McArthur's agrarianism and nationalism were strong. Consequently, such native creatures as red squirrels, woodchucks, raccoons, and even potato beetles played significant parts in some of his stories. Not all the fables centered in animals. A man of ingenious ideas, McArthur relished the chance the genre gave him to present strange situations. One of the best and most farfetched of these stories describes the plight of Jack Canuck, who cannot walk because his legs have quarreled. The moral, too, is surprising, for it asserts that this quarrel is no more silly than that between the country and the town, an unusual concession after all McArthur's years of fulminating against urban influences on the simple life.

II Cayuga Brook

Although McArthur wrote short fiction for only a few years, he never gave up his dream of producing an important novel. It started after his fall from grace as editor of *Truth*, when he decided to devote his time to fiction. Immediately he set to work on a comic novel. It was never published, but it did set a precedent, and the rest of his literary career is strewn with novels that he never published—some that he never finished and others that he mentioned but did not quite get down to writing. The comic novel *Cayuga Brook*, however, he did manage to complete. It runs to 179 manuscript pages and has, as McArthur justifiably boasted to Vaux, a "most ingenious plot," for the story centers on a very strange will. An eccentric businessman,

Cayuga Brook, leaves a dowry of one million dollars to any one
of the unmarried girls living in the town. It is, however, to be
given out only after all the girls have married and, according to a
secret clause disclosed after all have married, to the first of
them to become a widow. Shades of Mark Twain's "The Man
that Corrupted Hadleyburg"! McArthur could have done something here. The moral implications of the situation the will
could have engendered seem almost limitless, but McArthur
saw "no end to the comic situations" only.[11] The result is a
silly farce that has meaning only in its treatment of pioneer
social history of Western Ontario.

McArthur had been rusticating at Niagara-on-the-Lake while
working on his novel, and even before he had finished it he had
another in mind. He was "convinced that there [was] much
unbroken ground still left in the field of American fiction."[12]
Before the book had reached its final resting place, however,
almost three years later, filed under rejected, McArthur had, he
claimed, written the first three chapters nine times and the first
twelve, three times. Even taking account of McArthur's tendency to exaggerate, the numbers do indicate the accuracy of
his comment at the time, "I have the book idea bad."[13]

Lack of success dampened his enthusiasm, and before long
he was off on another tack and not until he reached England
did he return to novel writing. There among other vicissitudes
of fortune he met William T. ("T for Tumultuous," said Mc-
Arthur) Stead, who employed him to help with writing monthly
installments of a novel for Stead's *Review of Reviews*. Hack work
though the novel was, it does illustrate into what strange paths
McArthur's concern for letters led him. Begun in January, 1903,
and described as a Romance that was never to end, it required
its contributors to write the news of the world as fiction. They
were to use the main events of each month in a story centering
on the Gordon family, which comprised contemporary people
under false names. The identities of the originals of the fictitious
family were to remain secret, but the people from whom they
were drawn also appeared in the novel with their right names.
This tactic was adopted supposedly to throw the reader off the
scent, but actually to pique his curiosity and to turn the novel

into a *roman à clef*. The authors, for all their ingenuity, found the novel beyond them. Geography and time and the actuality of event and character made it almost impossible to put all together in a unified story, and the Romance that was never to end expired in Stead's *Daily Paper* little more than a year after the appearance of its first installment.

It is difficult to know exactly what McArthur, who joined Stead's group only in March, contributed to the novel, but Chapter XIII, "A Young Lochinvar From Canada," is certainly his. (Among other evidences it mentions the *Transcript* of Glencoe, Ontario.) Obviously McArthur all but forgot he was writing fiction, for the chapter reads like an essay in British-Canadian relationships, taking up matters such as weather, land settlement, remittance men, the influence of the United States on Canada, and class distinction, the last thinly disguised as an unacceptable love affair between the Canadian cousin and Mildred, a young English upper-crust lady and distant relative.

Thus ended "novel" number two, but failure never extinguished hope in a man as sanguine as McArthur. His ambition was merely banked, and it flared up again a decade later with a novel, again about pioneer life in Ontario. But it was the same old rigmarole. On October 8, 1911, McArthur told Vaux that he hoped to finish the book within a month, but as late as January, 1914, the complete novel was still only a hope, and it seems to have remained one. At least there is no extant manuscript. The same fate awaited two later books that appear to have caused only friction with their prospective publishers. Thomas Allen never did receive the manuscript of a novel called *Where Do We Go from Here?* (1920)—probably because it never existed. Nor could Lorne Pierce, editor of the Ryerson Press, ever get his hands on *The Frivolous Prince* that McArthur pegged away at for a year during 1922–23, but again without completing it.

A record of frustration, it may mean that McArthur simply did not know how a novel works and had little time to learn, what with farm work and three or four weekly articles to prepare. Yet he could create character; he knew how to tell a story; he had something to say. It may mean, then, as with his drama, that he was trying to work with the wrong formula, that he was trying to fit his material and his way of seeing into an inappropriate form. He complained that Canadian literature had not really dealt with farm life, but he read a novel, according to his own admission, by testing the first chapter for interesting characters and the last to see whether they live "happily ever after." If the ending is "one of the artistic kind that leaves everything up in the air or if the ending is tragic I lay the book aside and refuse to have my feeling[s] harrowed."[14] Moreover, he valued invention, humor, and plot highly. As a result he attempted to write fiction of farm life, which, false to his true understanding of it, made it impossible for him to handle his material satisfactorily, as *Cayuga Brook* and "Anywhere," the incomplete serialized romance in *Ourselves,* disclose. Romantic love, which he regarded as a necessary ingredient of his long fiction (and of many of his short stories), simply would not fit his view of or interest in the rural without falsifying both, his Victorianism or puritanism precluding everything but the sentimental or the comic, as if he were afraid to treat the subject squarely.

CHAPTER 3

Editor

I Scaling the Ladder

PETER McArthur kept or tried to keep a diary, during 1895 when he was living in New York, but like most diaries it soon began to falter and gave out completely by spring, struggling on only in the back pages as a record of debts and lists of groceries. Yet while it lasted it was more than a diary. It allowed McArthur to become his own confidant and confessor, for his puritan upbringing had taught him to keep a watch on himself. In it he almost continually upbraids himself. One day he writes, "Rather lazy. Intend to reform tomorrow," but the next day remorsefully tells his diary, "Have wasted another day and have about given up all hope of reform."

Aside from the nagging worry about lack of moral fiber, McArthur, like his fellow Bohemians, lived at the time, as he said, in a permanent state of temporary impecuniosity. His fortunes fluctuated between down and further down usually. On only two occasions in three months free-lancing was his weekly income above twenty dollars. So a fear that "laziness is now clothing me like a garment" was only balanced by his "feeling poverty-stricken." Then on March 16, the wheel turned and the diary reads exuberantly, "had a streak of industry today and completed 'An Amateur Crusoe,' a boy's story. Got a note from Tom Hall telling me that he has been appointed editor of *Truth*. Am going to pay a call on him tomorrow by his invitation. Feel that I did a day's work today. Best week yet."

II Truth

When McArthur made that entry in his diary, he little dreamed that it marked the beginning of his ambition to estab-

51

lish himself as a magazine editor, for the next day he visited
Hall, who, inviting him to become associate editor of the magazine, set him on a road that he tried to follow for sixteen years,
rough though it was. The diary records the first days of this
Odyssey and reads like a thriller: "I am not allowing myself to
be hopeful." "The plot is rapidly thickening in the Truth office." "Hall is victorious." "I hope to arrange for an assistant
editorship with him. I am not sure I'll be able to arrange it
though." "The Truth engagement is still hanging fire." Then
on Tuesday, April 9, there comes this entry, "Began work in
Truth office today."

Soon motes appeared in the beam, and the very next day
McArthur was informing the diary of his doubts about Hall's
ability as editor and, by Saturday, about the whole *Truth* enterprise. "The office is run so strangely and the paper is so expensive that I fear it can never be made to prosper." Yet though the
diary of two weeks later exclaims "Truth Troubles Still Heigho!"
McArthur weathered the storm and "in spite of all troubles and
wars" became editor in chief in July, 1895, when only twenty-
nine years old, though he had to wait until November, 1896, for
the pleasure of seeing his name on the masthead. Within a short
time, things were running smoothly, and, full of big schemes, he
saw himself, he told his wife in July, 1896, "as holding the job
for a long time." He little guessed that within a year, almost to
the very day, he would withdraw from the magazine, lock,
stock, and barrel, after a fierce quarrel in the upper offices.

Despite the fact that McArthur "liked a row" and that "the
commune" (the boardinghouse gang) had nicknamed him
"Huntin' Trouble," the squabble rankled him, not to mention the
loss of a job paying a posh one hundred dollars a week. Living a
life of enforced ease at his wife's home at Niagara-on-the-Lake
healed no wounds, and he turned to writing a series of "Bilious
Pete Ballads," one of which served as an abreaction to the *Truth*
affair. At least in the ballad he won.

> My brain has turned to tallow
>   And my guts are clogged with grease,
> My smile is bland and callow
>   And my presence reeks of peace;

> Yet the war dogs!—Once I sicced them
> On the fat-head folk with glee
> When Horton was the victim
> And Knapp the referee.[1]

Several years later, when once again enthusiastic about editorial work, with W. T. Stead's publications, McArthur was able to look back more dispassionately. Even if he were to surpass his "sky-rocket record" with *Truth* there would be "the difference that I now have a little sense."[2]

When McArthur joined the staff of *Truth*, it was but eight years old. It had begun as a publication of a small New York lithographic company, but had been taken over in 1890 by a new organization, the Truth Company, a branch of the American Lithograph Company, which had been formed that year by a merger of thirteen lithographic companies of New York, Buffalo, and Philadelphia. The company prospered and by the time McArthur became editor *Truth* was a weekly magazine of sixteen large, glossy pages (each 10" by 13") and sold at ten cents a copy or by subscription at five dollars a year.

Once appointed editor, McArthur soon adopted new-broomism as his policy. With typical gusto he proclaimed: "*Truth* takes pleasure in announcing to its patrons that on and after September 14 [1895], the paper will be enlarged and improved in every way. Besides the usual humorous and literary matter and colored cartoons, each issue will contain a picturesque article illustrated in colors. These articles will be written by clever writers, and all will deal with subjects of the liveliest interest. With the enlarged paper TRUTH will begin the publication of a series of pictures by celebrated artists, showing different phases of poker—the national game of America." The new editor concluded his statement with a firm resolution that "the new TRUTH will be clean, bright and entertaining. It will be filled from cover to cover with beautiful pictures, jokes, sketches, poems and stories; in short, it will be in every way the most interesting and readable publication in America."[3]

The colored pictures were, of course, the *raison d'être* of the publication, for, being the first magazine in the United States to carry photo color prints, it was intended largely as a way of advertising the work of the American Lithograph Company. So eager was the company to prove the merits of the new photo color printing process that it made the big center double-page color illustrations available, "on heavy paper suitable for framing," at fifty cents each or six for two dollars or in folios of twenty for five dollars. In addition the masthead held out this bait: "TRUTH is mailed to subscribers in strong paste-board tubes, and not folded, insuring the receipt of a clean, smooth paper, that will not be wrinkled or crumpled or otherwise damaged in the mails. This is for the convenience of the readers who wish to preserve a file of TRUTH or to frame the elegant double-page illustrations."

The cover always carried colored illustrations. The front usually pictured some billowy young beauty staring soulfully into space or ogling, or being ogled by, cupid, or a "summer girl" with tantalizing ankles riding a bicycle, or a "Chrysanthemum girl" in some elegant setting of flowers and pigeons. The back put on no such airs and carried bizarre cartoons, frequently with political implications, or advertisements of the latest bicycle tires. The magazine also contained dozens of black and white drawings to illustrate many of its innumerable jokes and often many of its poems and stories. Its last three pages were its bread-and-butter pages, which, likewise garnished with illustrations, were to tempt the reader with such wonders as "Fit and Misfit, Dr. Warner's Caroline Corsets." "Quick Puton Shirts," "Ball Bearing Bicycle Shoes," and "The Scorcher Bicycle."

McArthur saw the magazine as something other than a vehicle for advertising, and under him it had considerable literary and artistic merit. Its general tone was mildly satirical and its reading light, Leacock's kind of sketch or tale—"The Awful Fate of Melpomenus Jones" and "Boarding House Geometry" along with many other of his stories were published in it—exemplifying its kind of fiction; and facile romantic love or nature poetry, or *verse de société* and the flippant ballade, its kind of poetry. Editorials were short and, if political, pro-Republican. It had no section devoted to sport or to finance and business and carried no serial with the exception of A. Bigelow Paine's *The Dumpies,* a series of comic illustrations with a story in verse about animals and children.

Many of the contributions to the magazine were published anonymously, but one suspects the hand of McArthur in "Pen Points," a weekly column of epigrams. Anonymity disappears surely in face of comments such as "There is no use in hashing up old ideas. The joke that is well done is also rare" or "Hope is the influence that prejudices our views for the purpose of encouraging us." If these apothegms and dozens more like them are not from McArthur then someone must have borrowed the pen he had used in those years spent as a free-lancer concocting jokes and witty fillers for New York magazines and newspapers.

Busy as McArthur was as editor he found time to continue writing and published two poems and seven short stories in *Truth* and a series of five "Tales of Millionaires," each of which seemed to point to the folly of being one. He made innovations and tried to deemphasize the pictorial aspect of the magazine, withdrawing the notice from the masthead of the value of keeping the journal for the sake of framing its color prints. He introduced book reviews and a column on the New York theaters with himself as drama critic. He tried, also, to add interest with "An Innovation in Journalism," namely, "A Department for Deserving Domestic Animals," which was to comprise anecdotes about readers' pets. Either the readers had no pets or their pets never indulged in anecdotes, for "An Innovation in Journalism," after only three numbers, passed into oblivion, mercifully taking with it the name of its editorial supervisor, Josh M. A. Long. The series of "picturesque articles illustrated in colors" that the new editor introduced did not catch on, either, or perhaps the expense of producing it in addition to the regular four colored pages was too great for the company. Whatever the reason, the series ceased after eleven numbers, even though it belongs among the best work the magazine published under McArthur's aegis. One is tempted to see his hand in such articles as "The Daily Papers," "Up the Hudson," "The Fall Fair," and "Football," but, bearing no signatures, they cannot safely be ascribed to him.

The double center pictures of poker made a bigger hit. According to H. A. Bruce they were so successful that they caused the demise of the magazine, since the cost of production of many sets of colored illustrations proved unprofitable for the publishing enterprises taken as a whole.[4] At any rate they gained considerable acclaim for McArthur's fellow Canadian Jay Hambidge, who contributed among many other illustrations the popular *The Draw on the Bowery* with its subtitle "Where they draw from the spigot as often as they do from the deck." There is nothing of the sophisticated here, but rather a realistic picture of the seamy life of Bowery bums quite out of keeping with the rest of the center-fold illustrations, focused as they were on beautiful young women and handsome men of the upper crust.

If the magazine indulged in social criticism it confined its attack to the middle classes (although the cartoons often made fun of the beggar and the "nigger") and then to a satire of manners. If it went further it normally took up cudgels, albeit dainty ones, against big politicians and big capitalists.

Foreign rulers were fair game, especially the royal family of Germany, but not of England, as the *Sun* discovered when it derided Queen Victoria's Diamond Jubilee as the glorification of a person of "negative qualities." "*The Sun,*" an irate *Truth* replied, has only "positive qualities," but would be more acceptable "if it had a record for not being guilty of vituperation, of personal bias and vengefulness. . . ."[5] Apparently McArthur's Imperial spirit was roused and if in the Grub-Street war he could get in a few potshots at a rival, so much the better. A feeling for things British manifested itself more significantly, however, in McArthur's ready acceptance of contributions from Canadians.

McArthur knew some of the Canadian contributors to *Truth* personally—Jay Hambidge, Charles G. D. Roberts, Bliss Carman, Charles Jefferys. He had met them in New York, where they, like him, were trying to make good. Others he knew by correspondence—Archibald Lampman, Stephen Leacock, and Duncan Campbell Scott. Taken all in all, on an artistic level *Truth* to a large extent became a Canadian enterprise, a statement that can be made of no other magazine in the United States before or since the days when McArthur held sway at 203 Broadway Avenue in the mid-1890's.

Of all the Canadians, Jay Hambidge seems to have had an almost open sesame with no fewer than nine covers and twenty-four center-fold pictures to his credit in McArthur's day. It was not simply a case of Canadian nationalism, however, for Hambidge had a high contemporary reputation as an artist. Among the writers Leacock stood first with no fewer than eighteen contributions. Most have been republished, and Leacock has become recognized as an author of renown, the fact forgotten that he was once an unknown struggling for a place in the literary sun. Leacock never forgot, though, and long after paid tribute to the man who set him on the road to success by publishing him in *Truth*.

Roberts's poems (eleven all told) vary from simpering love lyrics celebrating the charms of an ethereal Phillida to some sturdy stanzas about life on a farm, and their acceptance by editor McArthur makes an excellent gauge of his own ambivalent attitude toward the nature of poetry. Like Roberts, Carman found *Truth* open to him. He discovered, also, even if McArthur inclined to look kindly on Canadians, his Bohemian years with McArthur did not outweigh other considerations. Carman submitted a poem of fifty stanzas. McArthur cut it to three and then informed the poet of what he had done. Carman accepted the reduction in size of the piece, but, to balance accounts, refused a reduction of his fifty-dollar fee.[6]

McArthur published only three poems by Lampman and four by Scott. Lampman by the mid-1890's had already established himself, so that McArthur was on fairly safe ground with him. Scott presented a somewhat different situation, for he had yet to make his name, and McArthur had only his own perspicacity as guide for the most part, but he did not hesitate. He honored the first publication of the notable poem "The Piper of Arll" with a two-page spread in the special Christmas (1895) number of the magazine and called on Hambidge to do the illustrations. One immediate result was that it "set on fire" a young Englishman named John Masefield, then working in Yonkers. Thus a Canadian poem, appearing in an American magazine (albeit through the agency of its Canadian editor), proved to have been also an important event in the annals of British poetry. McArthur always admired Scott and time has proved him right. Years later he paid this tribute to the old days he spent as editor of one of New York's most talked of nineteenth-century magazines. "If old

Truth," he confessed to his wife, "did nothing else for me it made me friends with Scott."

During McArthur's editorship, *Truth* had a unified tone and shape. It leaves the impression that all the contributors worked together with great good spirits, largely because it bears the stamp of one man. As a result the magazine has a personality that reflects the wit, kindliness, and intelligence of Peter Mc-Arthur on almost every page. Whatever brought on the quarrel between the editor and the business officers of the company, it could not have been his failure to produce a magazine of merit within its proper class.

III   Originator

Truth did much more for McArthur than make him a friend of Scott. It made him a friend of Jay Hambidge and fostered both his ambition to establish another magazine and his confidence in himself as businessman. His friendship and his ambition proved a will-o'-the-wisp, but at Amityville, where he and Hambidge were discovering the curve of beauty and the architectural principles involved in building the Parthenon, all was optimism. By 1902, Hambidge, now in England with plans for rebuilding the Greek ruin, sent back word that victory was theirs. Sir Francis Crammer Penrose, the head of the Greek department of the British Museum, not only accepted the Hambidge-McArthur theory, he "even apologized for some theories he has advocated in the past." It is "about time for Peter McArthur to enter," Hambidge continued,[7] and so he entered, lured by the promise of the editorship of a brand new magazine devoted to the cause and by a hankering to try his luck overseas, as he had been down at heel since leaving *Truth*.

McArthur set off for England in September, 1902. No sooner had he arrived than he rushed into the work of preparing the new magazine. Clouds began to gather quickly. First he had to select a title for the publication, but that required some knowledge of its subject matter. There was, too, the matter of financing it. For the first of these problems, McArthur soon found an answer. After "trying about fifty" titles, he lit on the name *Originator,* because it is, as he told Vaux in a letter of September

9 (1902), "so American and irritating" and "sounds as if it might
mean something, without meaning anything in particular and
will ... pique curiosity."[8] A little later, when he was more
definitely indefinite, he boasted that the magazine was "glor-
iously indefinite," for he was, as business manager and editor,
"free," he said, "to originate anything from a row to a Reform
wave."[9] He could not know then how prophetic he was, for the
first of the alternatives the *Originator* certainly did originate.

That event was to come later. Now that he had settled on a
title, he had the problem of setting out an editorial policy. He
had chosen as subtitle "the magazine of attainable ideals." Now
he had to explain what ideals he meant and how they were
attainable. He feared that the title might offend with its suggestion of sacredness when the magazine was to be entirely
secular. He consoled himself, nevertheless, in a letter of October
2 to Vaux, by pointing out that the word "originator" had "never
been used in a sacred sense. . . . It may convey a sense of cheek . . .
and the cheek I think I can live down or live up to." Moreover,
he prided himself that the title was justifiable, since he had
made it a policy to "originate an advertising idea" for any who
advertised in the magazine, and, setting the rate at ten pounds
per page, he was soon dreaming and talking of an income of a
hundred and twenty pounds a year from every page set aside for
his "ideas." The "originate an idea scheme" he believed firmly
not only took "the curse off the name of the magazine," but
also meant much money in the bargain.[10]

He worried, also, over the scientists and artists, for the magazine centered on teaching the law of form, and he sometimes
thought the whole thing a frightening gamble. Yet there was to
be no happy medium. As usual with McArthur, with any new
project he fluctuated between high enthusiasm and soul-destroy-
ing doubt and saw himself as the leader of a crusade "that will
bring us the highest success" or we will "be laughed out of
court."[11] To obviate the latter embarrassment he aimed at producing a magazine "outside the idea of teaching the law of form—
a paper, in fact, that can live it down should the law of form
be exploded—though I think there is little danger of that, if
it is properly presented."[12]

There are straws of disaster in the wind here, too. One of the men helping to finance the magazine stepped heavily on Mc-Arthur's toes by asking whether this young editor understood the philosophy it was to teach. He found that McArthur did and "that the Lord," as McArthur later told his wife, "did not put the poison of asps under my tongue for nothing." Finally the storm subsided, and the magazine made a start. By hook and by crook, McArthur wangled five hundred pounds to finance the first three numbers and a promise of five thousand pounds more "if things appear to be going smoothly."[13] For the moment Hambidge and he would content themselves with the nominal salaries of four pounds a week each. He had rented two rooms at Outer Temple, Strand, set January 1, 1903, as a deadline, and began sending out letters proudly bearing in heavy black print across the top the full title like a banner, "The *Originator* / A magazine of atttainable ideals," with the names of the two editors neatly tucked in at the side of the page. And that was all there ever was to the magazine. Hambidge became involved with the Hellenic Society and had only time to pick up his *Originator* salary, so that McArthur soon became peeved to find that his high-sounding title of business manager was an inclusive term for office boy, odd-jobs man, and advertising agent.

The real trouble, however, derived from the editorship. Mc-Arthur had come to doubt the mathematical as a basis for aesthetics. Art entailed feeling also. Hambidge held for his theory of dynamic symmetry and went on to develop it in lectures and books. McArthur went on to develop his concept of art—far removed from Hambidge's—in his essays and poems. The quarrel between the two men had more immediate effects. Hambidge departed for the United States, taking three hundred pounds with him, which, according to McArthur, belonged to Mr. Taylor, the man who had financed the abortive undertaking and whom Hambidge had the effrontery to call a cad when called to account for his actions.

By the time of the breakup of the Amityville school of philosophy McArthur had already begun dickering with Robert Barr for a position on the *Idler* magazine. McArthur asserts that Barr offered him some kind of place, but, if he did, nothing came of it, McArthur's dislike of Barr probably playing some part in his failure to join the magazine. Shortly McArthur became business manager of W. T. Stead's *Daily Paper*, but it failed almost immediately and before long McArthur gave up his conquest of Britain and returned to the United States and finally to Ekfrid. Scarcely had he reached there, however, than he began dusting off his old ambition to establish a magazine.

IV Ourselves

This one would be free from the risk of unsympathetic financiers. Nor would the editor have to chafe under the restraint of partners and editorial committees, for by making himself both president and editor McArthur would remove all such nuisances. Impetuously as ever he "was rushing headlong into a new venture," he informed Vaux in September, 1910, and "the indications are that it will be a success. . . . it was announced only last Saturday, but subscriptions are coming in by every mail."

The cause of the excitement was no big sophisticated magazine centering on color illustrations and sophisticated New York society, no *Originator* dedicated to the dissemination of aesthetic theory. It was a little magazine, *Ourselves*, which like many others of its kind in Canada, lived but a short life, despite the enthusiastic announcement of its birth. Anemic from the start, for it began "without a cent of capital," it lingered through seven numbers between October, 1910, and June, 1911. Subscribers and wished-for subscribers were warned of its coming demise in an advertisement, which, however, did hold forth the hope that if borrowers of the magazine would only subscribe it would "have the largest circulation of any magazine in Canada." Whatever alarm resulted from these distress signals, the legion of borrowers failed to leap into the breach, and *Ourselves* gasped its last in April, 1912, in a final number (eight) after almost a nine-month coma. Whatever the grounds for confidence at the beginning, McArthur made no bones about what he thought were the causes for its failure in these disturbing accusations. "The powers have done all they could to suppress it. They refused it ordinary mailing privileges and the news company stopped handling it and they got my publisher to refuse to publish it unless I brought it out as a straight Liberal paper."[14] This at least is the story that wailing-wall Vaux had to listen to.

This discussion is to anticipate, however, for *Ourselves*, "A magazine for Cheerful Canadians," began with a flourish. Although the format was small (5" x 6½"), the name in a gold-colored panel and fifty pages of text, concluding with a chapter from *To Be Taken With Salt: Being an Essay on Teaching One's Grandmother to Suck Eggs*, the ill-starred book he had published in England, demonstrate what a bargain the magazine was intended to be at ten cents a copy. Moreover, the editor had managed to drum up three pages of advertisements. The magazine contained no statement of editorial policy, but its general political bias became clear immediately, for the first of McArthur's regular column "The Monthly Talk" opened *in medias res*. "This is a word for word report of a political argument I heard one day:

" 'He didn't!'

" 'He did!'

" 'He didn't!'

" 'He did!' "

This conversation between two "leading citizens, a Liberal and a Conservative (they [were] really too important to be called a Grit and Tory),"[15] makes an excellent substitute for a policy statement, especially when read along with the following quotation from Agnes Kingston with which the magazine opens, since together they indicate the general tone, attitude, and subject matter that was to be the magazine's throughout. "My Love for Canada is bound up with my respect for the Commandment 'Honour thy father and thy mother' My father and mother hewed out a home for themselves in Canada, they are laid at rest here and I ask that my days may be long in the land."[16]

Ourselves aimed at being a rural magazine. The many articles on politics and economics were to defend the rights of the farmer against urban forces, and the studies of pioneer life, which formed a regular feature of the publication, were to inculcate values and foster a love of country life and, more generally, Canadian nationalism.

The first issue of *Ourselves* was almost a solo flight—the editor contributing nine of the ten items listed in the formidable table of contents—and so it remained. McArthur could not pay contributors, but he did get some help from Clayton Duff with a pleasant bucolic essay, "A Field Day," and a poem, "The Call of the Wild." Leacock's "My Financial Career" (reprinted from *Life*), Arthur Phelps's poem "The Monk of Abbey Blanc," and an excerpt from David Kennedy's *Pioneer Days* also helped to lighten McArthur's burden, but the number of contributors remained almost nil. Of a total of seventy-four pieces published in the magazine, sixty-one (or put in other terms, 374 of 419 pages) were McArthur's.

As a result the overtaxed editor simply plagiarized himself as a solution to his problem, not only serializing *To Be Taken With Salt*, but dicing its tenth chapter into his beloved epigrams for fillers. He went to *Truth* for a short story, "An Experiment with Wisdom," and his fine satirical tale "A Moral Bully," took poems from *The Prodigal and Other Poems* and various magazines, and began printing as a serial his pioneer novel *Anywhere*, "the Romance of a Puzzled Knight Errant in quest of an interest in life." Unfortunately it ceased in number seven, leaving the hero, Dan, who in keeping with an old romantic dodge had returned incognito to the old farm, forever on the threshold of love with the lovely heroine. "Continued in the next issue" helped not at all, probably because McArthur never completed the novel, or perhaps the long interval between June, 1911, and April, 1912, proved too great a barrier for the lovers. At any rate the rest is silence, for number eight contains not one word of *Anywhere*, it having lost place to "Kitty McBean," in which the heroine is again doomed in another incomplete romance to everlasting spinsterhood.

McArthur turned adversity to good account. The lack of contributors gave him the chance to have his say about the bygone days of the pioneers, which he loved, for they were the days of his childhood, and which he could return to vicariously through essays celebrating events and people of the past or use as the criteria for his satire of the present. Each issue of the magazine carried something about them, either as an article or tale, or as a short comment under "Told as New," a section devoted to jokes and a regular feature of all numbers, except number eight. Number one introduced the first of the essays by a pioneer, who was none other than McArthur himself. He knew the cut and gait of the early settlers and he knew how to tell a tale.

Only in the accounts of pioneer life and "Told as New" did
Ourselves generally fulfill its mission as "a magazine for cheerful
Canadians," for it carried not only the very serious feature, "The
Monthly Talk," but another politically-oriented regular column,
"The People's Editorial." The latter, supposedly participatory as
a sort of rendering of letters from readers, came obviously from
the pen of the editor on most occasions and can hardly have
cheered its readers with its comments about the chicaneries of
bankers and politicians. McArthur admitted his failing and
opened the third number with this admonition: "Some friendly
critics think that we have altogether too much politics in *Ourselves*. Very well! I am going to try to keep the dreadful stuff out
of this number." The dreadful stuff, alas, was in his blood, and
even this article develops into another attack on "Big Business
and little politics."

In the early numbers politics and cheerful Canadianism did
occasionally go hand in hand. Nothing in Leacock's *Sunshine
Sketches of a Little Town* surpasses the burlesque "Jim Cook's
Vote" and "The Row in the North Riding" for high-spirited genial
political satire, and "My Neighbor the Corporation," cut from
the same cloth, comes close to matching them. By the time this
sketch had appeared, however, McArthur had set the magazine
on a course that took it further into the polemics of economic
and political dispute and had begun to advertise "The Striking
Series of Articles on the Banking System in Canada."

McArthur realized that *Ourselves* was losing ground. He
pleaded with his readers. "Ten dollars will pay for a life subscription," states one advertisement. He flattered them (and
the magazine) with this felicitation: "The individuality of the
magazine" did "not appeal to the hoi polloi" of Canadians. He
was clutching at straws and he knew it; yet either because he
was determined to ride his own hobbyhorse or because his
enthusiasms blinded him to those of others, he finally turned his
magazine into a firing range in which an angry McArthur kept
up an almost incessant barrage against his favorite bogeymen,
the bankers, entrepreneurs, and politicians of the urban world,
in thumbnail sketches or long closely reasoned essays such as
"The Canadian Banking Combine," which spread over thirty-
two pages of the final issue of the journal.

Although any assessment of McArthur's attempts to produce a little magazine becomes for the most part a study of him as essayist, the subject of a subsequent chapter, something needs to be said of his work as editor. His first attribute was industry and dedication to a cause. In the old days these qualities helped him to rise rapidly to the position of editor of a periodical that held its own in the severely competitive New York market. *Ourselves* demonstrates, also, an independence of mind that in *Truth* expressed itself in light social satire (and McArthur's resignation), but that here apparently led to a public confrontation with strong political powers. There are shades of *Truth* (and a half dozen similar magazines of the 1890's) in the pages of humorous tidbits in *Ourselves*. Editor McArthur had apprenticed himself to such magazines and, for him, jokes, funny anecdotes, and cartoons were necessary ingredients of any magazine that was aimed at the general public. In *Truth* he could call on any number of talented people for such material. *Ourselves* had to depend on its editor for its jokes and on *To Be Taken With Salt* for its cartoons; yet the idea persisted that such things were essential. Somehow the humor seems an addendum. The magazine seems to try to be a *Truth* on the one hand and a learned journal on the other, what had been light social satire in the one giving way to heavy social criticism in the other.

Ourselves is not proof of McArthur's powers of criticism, except self-criticism. Nor could it open the door to Canadian writing as *Truth* had been able to. An empty editorial purse scarcely interested the established authors. For all that, McArthur never suggested an all-come-all-served editorial policy. That he published little other than his own work might also indicate critical standards that refused publication to many would-be contributors. The problems went deeper than purse and aesthetics. *Ourselves*, now a curiosity in the literary history of Canada, manifests something of what stood between McArthur and his ambition to establish his reputation as a magazine editor. His strength was his weakness. He allowed his enthusiasm to become an obsession and failed to keep a balanced view. At home probably in a periodical devoted solely to some particular—politics or economics—he seems not to have had the detachment required for a magazine of a general nature. *Our-*

selves is brilliant at times, but leaves the overall impression that it was basically a mouthpiece for aggressive social criticism.

This quality was not enough to keep it alive, for as it narrowed in scope it narrowed in interest, and undoubtedly also antagonized some readers with sufficient background to follow its arguments. Moreover, McArthur had begun to find the newspaper more suited to his talent and his way of life. Success with the *Globe* and the *Farmer's Advocate* need not take him from his farm, which he realized more and more was the inspiration of his best work. As essayist he was free from all the niggling affairs that editing had entailed. As farmer-essayist he had the best of both worlds and as farmer-essayist he made his reputation; and *Ourselves* remains an interesting bypath that he took momentarily on his way to his impressive achievements as chronicler of rural life.

CHAPTER 4

Biographer and Critic

I The Making of a Biography

ALTHOUGH *Sir Wilfrid Laurier* (1919) is the only biography McArthur published, he produced sketches and profiles throughout his career as a writer. By bent of mind he found biography congenial. Like Josh Billings, it pleased him, he said, because it enabled us to " 'compare the great man's virtues with our own and his faults with our neighbour's.' " Actually he liked it because, above all else, he was a humanist and hence inquisitive about man's activities. Ideas and things tended to interest him most when they put on flesh and blood or related directly to daily life. For him the "isms" and movements of the past were largely a matter of the adventures and accomplishments of such men as Tiger Dunlop, Colonel Talbot, Neil McAlpine, and the individual exploits of those other pioneers

> [Who] bore themselves like men of might
>   At work—and at the table!
> They chopped and burned—and cheered their souls
>   With many a deep potation!
> They bore themselves by night and day
>   Like builders of a nation.[1]

If McArthur thought of the past mainly in terms of individuals, and of history as biography for the most part, he saw contemporary Canada in much the same way. With its mergers, trusts, and power politics, it was largely the shadow of its Max Aitkenses, Clifford Siftons, and Sir Sam Hugheses, the world symbolized by the fictional and pompous Sir Jingo McBore, about whom McArthur had once intended writing a novel, but whom he eventually relegated to the lesser genre of the limerick.

67

Once, too, he even wrote a story entitled "My Neighbor the Corporation," which ended disastrously for the hero when, "in a burst of neighbourly good fellowship," he invited the merger to go fishing with him, only to get a letter from merger's lawyer. In larger and more abstract matters such as the meaning of democracy and the significance of Canadian nationalism, two favorite topics, he was less concerned with theory than with the characters of the nation's leaders and its people.

Although McArthur often interprets history as the shadow of men who impose their wills on others, he saw in Sir Wilfrid Laurier no such man but one who, as a true statesman, expressed in both word and deed the values of democracy and nationalism as McArthur defined them. He admired the man who once addressed an audience at Winnipeg with these words of hope:

In the thirty years that I have led the Liberal party, my platform has always been Canada first. Whether on one side or another, on this question or that, my guiding star has always been my Canadian country. There is a crisis, and we must fight on as fought the pioneers of the early days in Canada, the strong, stern men who kept in sight their goal of Canada's best interests against all difficulties and obstacles. Let our motto be the same as theirs—"Fortitude in Distress." There are breakers ahead, but we shall reach the shore if we fight on. We can bring to pass in Canada what was prophesied by a distinguished American once—that the twentieth century would be the century of Canada.[2]

For the most part McArthur's apprentice work in biography before *Sir Wilfrid Laurier* appeared comprised the short essays he contributed to the *Globe* and to his own magazine, *Ourselves*. In the latter he ran a column called "Who's Who" and presented sketches of seven Canadian leaders including Henri Bourassa and Sir Wilfrid Laurier. These hint at McArthur's methods as biographer in general and demonstrate his concern that political leaders understand their relationships to those led:

All public men are really characters in fiction. What they really are and really do does not matter so much as what people believe about them. It is useless for the papers and magazines to write them up and try to give an exact impression of them as they are. The pictures of them that will live are those that the public make up from odds and ends of information.

In order to give public men some idea of their "form and pressure" on the public mind it is proposed to give from time to time brief character sketches, the information for which is gathered from the plain people rather than from press agents. These sketches will be written less for information and amusement of the public than for the enlightenment of those who are described.[3]

It is doubtful whether the subjects of the sketches were ever much enlightened by them, but McArthur here anticipated the modern concern with the public image and tried to inform the leaders of their status with the populace. "Sir Wilfrid Laurier" is far less enthusiastic about the Liberal leader than McArthur's later study, and, like irony that lacks a clearly defined base, it may have left questions about the intention of the author. He depicted Sir Wilfrid as a man who "if he has to do any injury to a political opponent . . . is as polite about it as the comic opera villain who invariably said: 'Excuse me while I stab you,' " and also as a man to whom one could apply "Goldsmith's simile. Though the rolling clouds of politics about his breast are spread, 'Eternal sunshine settles on his head.' And," he continues, "if in depicting this phase of our first citizen the cartoonists show a comic high-light where the sunshine touches his bald spot it is only an evidence of the sportive exuberance of a young and growing nation."[4] As a journalist McArthur ought to have known the risk he ran of being misconstrued in writing of this kind. Grits reading the sketch could hardly be sure that the reference to a shining bald spot was "sportive exuberance" as the author claimed, but the Tories were certain about the parts that praised Sir Wilfrid.

Aside from an innate interest in biography, McArthur brought to bear on his work a long association with the Liberal party and a personal friendship with Laurier. McArthur had Liberalism in his bones, for the family had been Liberals from the very beginning, and from the moment he returned to Canada he cast his fortunes with the Liberal cause. A long-time friend, Alex Smith, an Ottawa lawyer and the National Liberal Organizer, appointed him manager of the federal Liberal election campaign of 1908. He knew of McArthur's work with *Truth,* of his hectic

three or four months as advertising manager of W. T. Stead's
Daily Paper, and of the Ryder-McArthur Publicity Agency of
New York to which McArthur had given much time, work, and
enthusiasm for three years following his return from Europe
in 1904. Nor was Smith disappointed, for McArthur pepped up
the Liberal electioneering with a strong injection of hoopla.
Despite its success, it was a few years later, however, to con-
tribute this little scene to Canadian political history.

He [McArthur] beckoned me [E. C. Drury] to a chair beside him.
"Come here, Drury," he said. "I've a confession to make, for I have
done a hellish thing and it will work 'em woe. 'Twas I who introduced political advertising into Canada. Ah, 'twas an evil thing!
Do you remember the last election [1908], the posters on the bill-
boards and the full-page advertisements in the newspapers, and
the pictures of Laurier driving a railroad spike? And the little verse
         Work, work, work, let Laurier finish his work
         And talk, talk, talk, let Borden keep on his talk!
'Twas I who did it all."[5]

Despite the lament, McArthur never abated his faith in the
Liberals. He defended the Naval Bill (1910) and Reciprocity,
the Achilles heel of the Liberal party in the election of 1911,
and when Laurier lost it McArthur became a watchdog for the
party. He stood ready at all times to rush to an attack on the Conservatives, whom he invariably identified with Big Business, or
to defend Laurier against the blue-blooded Imperialists, who
mistook his stand against military conscription in 1917 as tanta-
mount to treason. Indeed, late in life McArthur had become so
well acquainted with the "Old Chief" that he played the role of
minor consultant, as he informed Vaux in a letter of September
30, 1916. "After my Montreal speech I went to Ottawa and had
a long interview with Sir Wilfrid Laurier in which we were
in entire agreement on all questions of public policy. He was
afraid to come out against imperialism, but after our talk he
made a speech in Montreal in which he stated his opposition
clearly. He also asked me to go to parliament to support him,
but I declined. . . . But it is hard to resist the blandishments of
so charming a leader as Sir Wilfrid when he tells me he wants
me in parliament." Later, in a letter of May 26, 1918, he informed

his son, Daniel, that Sir Wilfrid sent for him, wanting him to go to Ottawa to spend a day with him to talk things over, and even to the end this close relationship continued, for within a week or two of the death of the "Old Chief" McArthur received an invitation to visit him.

II   Sir Wilfrid Laurier

McArthur was, then, well qualified by these experiences as well as his other attributes to write Laurier's biography, and when, shortly after Laurier's death (February 19, 1919), the opportunity to do so came, McArthur took it. At the time only two significant studies of Laurier were available: One, Sir John Willison's *Sir Wilfrid Laurier and the Liberal Party* (1903), and the other, O. D. Skelton's *The Day of Sir Wilfrid Laurier* (1916). There was a need, and it was time, for a more complete biography, and J. M. Dent and Sons recognizing this need called on Peter McArthur to fill it. They had already published him and knew that he and Laurier were well acquainted. They knew that the market was there if they struck while the iron was hot. They wanted a book in a hurry, and McArthur wrote it for them in a hurry, beginning March 5 and finishing on March 19, 1919. In the intimacy of a letter to Daniel, he confessed that he accepted a "rush order from Dent's" as a "mortagage lifter" and boasted that "in doing a 200 page life of Laurier in two weeks I have knocked Toronto cold. It is the biggest stunt I ever did and I think the best."[6]

McArthur felt more deeply about Laurier than the letter implies and he aimed at more than a "mortgage lifter." He wished to record his admiration for a leader whose "one motive . . . was . . . the exaltation of Canada . . . and the subversion of all petty and sectional antagonisms," "the true imperialist, who saw this Empire as a voluntary confederation of free nations,"[7] views dear to McArthur's own heart. On another level he wanted to pay tribute to the man himself—to his love of children, his interest in nature, his dedication to learning, and to his personal charm and dignity of bearing. The book is not a biography in the usual sense of the word, but rather an appreciation of the dead leader. Even then it is unconventional in its methods. McArthur called

it "an experiment that startled the critics" and that led several
to compare it "to a narrative of one of the knights of King
Arthur's Round Table."[8] Later he described his experiment as
an "anthology of tributes" to Laurier. Both assessments have
merit. McArthur certainly presents him as a great and noble
man and as a true knight in court and among his people.
Though he disapproved of titles for Canadians, he believed the
knighthood conferred on Sir Wilfrid a justified honor for so
worthy a candidate.

McArthur's study was not so original as he thought, for it
follows the Victorian concept of biography closely. He considered biography the story of a great person in which only the
subject's virtues are discussed. He wanted to show Laurier at
his best, as a hero in a romance and as a model in political
morality and skill. In this he succeeded, one reviewer com-
mending him highly for impressing upon Canadians "the value
of good manners in a public career and the proof that they are
always the product of a cultivated understanding and a finished
taste. . . ."[9]

In presenting this spotless hero, McArthur ran the risk of
creating a prig and so destroying the reader's credulity and
interest, since the everlasting good becomes unbelievable and
boring. Yet he ran the risk successfully, although Laurier's moralizing speeches to the young and the windy rhetoric of some of
his public addresses present a challenge to the modern reader.
He is likely to chalk up a mark, not so much against Laurier,
however, as against McArthur for the uncritical enthusiasm
with which he quotes them. McArthur is right in speaking of
his book as an anthology of tributes, for it comprises dozens of
excerpts from Laurier's speeches (largely on colonial relationships and Canadian nationalism) and as many comments from the
press, for in his hurry he had to substitute a clipping service for
research. McArthur recognized his debt to the Canadian press
in a dedication admitting that he had "stolen much," and that
had he had more time he would "have stolen more."

McArthur replaced the traditional chronological pattern of
the biography with a mosaic under headings such as "Personal
Characteristics," "Feats of Memory," "The Grand Manner," and,
of course, McArthur's beloved "Anecdotes," aimed at catching

the man in action. This technique enabled McArthur to present a living portrait, for he struck a compromise between the static of the picture and the dynamic of words. By deemphasizing the flow of time he helped focus attention on the man himself. McArthur selected his material carefully so that he could illustrate Laurier's charm, courage, and high seriousness—though Laurier must rest a bit uneasily to know that one American newspaper referred to him as one of the greatest names "in the history of the sister republic."[10]

Occasionally McArthur himself steps forward to explain some matters pertaining to Laurier the politician—a catalogue of his achievements from 1896 to 1911, his fight for Reciprocity, his role in the Federal Union Government, which the Liberals and Conservatives formed for a short time during World War I, and the election campaign of 1917—or to dramatize or report some experience of his own. In this way he adds highlights to the portrait and shifts from the public to the private image of the man. For this McArthur needed no research. He had only to draw on memory for such an important biographical detail as this episode presents:

When I reached [Laurier's] home on Laurier Avenue, he was waiting for me, and although I had never met him before, his welcome was so simple and kindly that I felt at home at once, and felt as if we had been life-long friends. In a sense we had been, for I had admired him since I had first seen him on a platform over thirty years ago. . . .

But though his greeting made me feel not only at ease but flattered and happy, it was not long before I noticed something that aroused an old-time critical attitude. It so happened that many years ago I had served my time as a dramatic critic, and had learned to notice the little niceties by which an actor achieves his affects [*sic*]. Now I do not wish to accuse Sir Wilfrid of being an actor, but if his methods were spontaneous and merely happened so, they were still worthy of Booth, Irving or Belasco.

I was shown to his sitting-room, where a grate fire was burning. After a most cordial greeting, in which he referred to some of my activities, which had attracted his attention and pleased him, he motioned me to a chair and when I had seated myself he sat down beside me. While standing he towered over me in height, but to my surprise, when he sat down I was looking down into his earnest, attentive face. I instantly noticed that the chair on which he sat was several inches lower than the one on which I sat. The stage trick was so apparent that although I did not betray the fact that I had noticed it, it made me keenly alert for anything else of the same kind that might happen. For over an hour we engaged in a most animated conversation. . . .

Finally, he rose as if some thought had suddenly occurred to him. He walked over to the open fireplace, and stood with his back to me for a few moments. As he rose from the low chair on which he had been sitting and stood erect his heighth [sic] seemed more than mortal. Standing with his back to me, he seemed absorbed in profound thought, but presently he turned and his whole manner had changed. Instinctively I came to attention and stood before him. With the smile which made his followers adore him, he began abruptly.

Now, Mr. ——, what I want to know is what constituency are you going to contest in the coming election? . . .

Though I was deeply moved by the compliment implied by his request, the dramatic critic was still alert at the back of my head and chuckling with inward appreciation. The scene had been worthy of Booth at his best. Cardinal Richelieu could not have surpassed him. As a matter of fact, I have always thought of him since as "the Cardinal," and have used that title when speaking of him to intimate friends.

Though I had other interviews with him, none of them equalled the first in the exquisite attention to detail in the stage setting—the low chair, the open fireplace and the turning towards me with infinite suavity and appeal to make his request.[11]

If McArthur's friendship with Laurier and unbounded admiration for him and his brand of liberalism were a source of strength in the book, they were also responsible for some of its weaknesses. Of course like most anthologies it "suffered from omissions." It contained little or nothing on Laurier's involvement in such contentious political issues as Canada's role in the Boer War, Bourassa and French-Canadian nationalism, or the Navy Act of 1910. Since McArthur was sketching a man more than analyzing the actions of a politician the omissions may pass, especially since he takes up the very significant issues of Laurier's stand against church domination of state and his stand for Canadian unity at home and Canadian autonomy within the Empire. McArthur's errors of commission, however, can plead no such reservations, except enthusiasm for a cause and his own bent.

McArthur had recognized the problem of objectivity when he himself became the subject of Deacon's study. "I wonder what kind of person he will make me seem," he told Vaux. "We always, of necessity, create other people in our image and I suspect that he will portray himself as he finds himself expressed in my work. In spite of himself, . . . he will really portray his own inner self. . . . As I have now put together two biographies, Laurier and Leacock, I know how inescapably a man puts himself in that kind of book."[12] The Laurier whom Mc-Arthur, as a Protestant and Anglo-Saxon, depicted most appreciatively was, then, the Laurier who challenged the authority of the Roman Catholic Church in the school systems of the prairie provinces and preached freedom in a unified Canada, loyalty to the Empire, and the dawn of the People's Day in a New Democracy. " 'The race is open to all. Any man may come to this land who is willing to work. It matters not who his father was or from what land he came, or at what altar he bows, he can aspire to the best and the highest this land has to offer. Whatever a Briton-born can claim he may claim. British institutions know no difference whatever.' "[13]

McArthur never recognized in his admiration for Laurier one jot of the French-Canadian Nationalists' arguments. He quotes no French-Canadian newspapers and no French obituary. He had lectured on "Hyphenated Canadianism," in which he deplored the use of the terms French-Canadian, English-Canadian, Scotch-Canadian, since all are Canadians. In *Sir Wilfrid Laurier,* except for two quotations in which Laurier implies that Canada is a mosaic rather than a melting pot, McArthur unconsciously takes the same stand as in his lecture, not realizing that dropping the hyphen for a majority in Canada is one thing, that for a minority it is quite another.

The Laurier whom McArthur as farmer stressed is the man who spoke for free trade, that agrarian shibboleth and alleged panacea for all rural ills. Laurier even became a springboard from which McArthur launched into a long discussion of the prosperity that had resulted from Laurier's reduction of tariffs in the early twentieth century. Combining this panegyric with more than a hint that the reelection of the Liberal party would restore those palmy days, he occasionally came close to turning his book into a platform for a Liberal rally. Ignoring such matters as the questionable need for the two transcontinental railways built during Laurier's regime and the relationship of the opening of the continental west to the good times the country enjoyed when the Liberal party held office from 1896 to 1911, he proved that Laurier could do no wrong.

If Laurier were to play his role of knight successfully he had need of some dragon on which to break a lance, and that monster McArthur found in Conservatism. In all, however, it gave McArthur a greater opportunity to have his say than to discuss Laurier. Beginning with an epigram, "when a man becomes satisfied he becomes a Tory," the commentary spreads over the next twenty or so pages and, after a sprinkling of judgments such as "Liberalism has its principles embodied in the human heart," and "In the case of Liberalism the emphasis has usually been on the 'common good,'" he arrives at a conclusion equating Liberalism with progress and democracy.[14] For all the talk of the masses and the need to move ahead, however, McArthur is closer to what he considers the Conservative position than he realizes, and it is largely Laurier's recognition of the value of tradition that forms the intellectual and emotional center of the biography. For McArthur, Laurier represented the last hope of ruralism and the chance to preserve some of the old ways in a world where the urban and industrial had already gained so much.

III   *Coming to Terms with Literature*

McArthur published relatively little literary criticism before writing *Stephen Leacock* (1923), a book now recognized as a superior study of the famous Canadian humorist. Yet it is scarcely an exaggeration to say he had unknowingly spent his life preparing for such a work. He was a humorist himself and had practiced his art over many years. Besides, through wide and continued reading since his childhood, he had laid a firm foundation for his kind of criticism, an informal and personal discussion normally of the characters and theme of a book, and sometimes of the author as revealed in it. Criticism was not merely a matter of opinions. Its basis was the book and its facts. He might agree with Swinburne that we must glow for these lovely things, but not without understanding why. As proof of his stand on impressionistic criticism there are his comments on Shakespeare and his other idol William Wordsworth.[15]

At times McArthur, the farmer, was such a severe critic of literature that books themselves were suspect. "We are inclined to make too much of books," he admonishes in an essay in *In Pastures Green* (p. 72), and, in a short story, "McPherson the Psychologist," Preston, a clever young man from the city, who "had been spoiled only by books," returns home, free of "his pride of knowledge" and aware "that men are more than books...."[16] Anti-intellectual as these observations are, in context they illustrate quite clearly the general grounds on which McArthur approached the criticism of literature. When he writes "we are inclined to make too much of books," he discloses the extreme of his tendency to make the societal the basis of criticism—in this comment, unconsciously, his pioneer background and, consciously, his fear that books blind the young to the values of the rural world and the beauty of nature and finally lure them away from the farm. In his observation about young Preston, he attacks intellectual snobbery, which he hated, and its complement, the fiction that presents the country man as rube.

McPherson, the hero of the story, the man who opened Preston's eyes to nature and man, symbolizes another pioneer belief in natural and unlettered ability. Although McPherson had studied books but little, he knew men; so what he said was a revelation to professors of "political economy" and was "too human to be compared with the evidence collected by eminent psychologists."[17] Obviously McPherson, modeled on the romantic native genius, had little use for the newfangled social sciences as approaches to criticism. One simply knew certain things and that they were beyond rational and cut-and-dried explanations. Obviously, to judge a book, if books were acceptable at all, one must compare it with life and not assess it in terms of theories about human behavior.

A strong personal element could and often did enter McArthur's criticism, as the comments cited suggest. Written when

he first returned to the farm, they manifest his enthusiasm for
his new way of life. Like Wordsworth, when he went back to his
childhood home, McArthur, in the early years of his return to
the farm, became a proselytizer for nature as opposed to books,
viewing the latter as symbols of the urban world in the everlasting and romantic debate of city against country. Despite all
disclaimers of books, McArthur realized, however, they were
only partly true. His whole life proved that nature was not
enough and that he cherished books dearly. He knew that he
believed in great literature also, and, perhaps in his heart,
believed that it alone revealed the truth about life. His love of
Shakespeare, to give a particular example, substantiates the
point, and, on another level, there is his essay "Reading for
the Country," which bemoans the lamentable state of rural
libraries.[18]

Much of this ambivalence derived from McArthur's convic-
tion that art must be didactic. He saw literature in terms of
content and paid little heed to it as an art form. In the truest
sense, then, if he felt deeds superior to words and nature superior
to books, he should have become a man of action rather than a
man of letters; but faced with the paradox of using words to
deny the validity of words, he chose to continue to use them,
an approach that did much to direct his discussion to what words
are used for rather than how they are used. Expression was a
matter of self-expression and spontaneity; a book was a form
of confession. The heroine of *Cayuga Brook* complains when discussing Canadian literature that "our writers think English
should be written as carefully as a dead language, while I claim
that it should be written so that people will feel sure that the
writer is alive."[19]

For McArthur, morality in art means "purity" as well as
didacticism. In a review of Arthur Stringer's *The Prairie Mother*,
he praised it, but found it flawed by being "a little too revealing about the intimacies of women."[20] When he commented on
the movies he came out strongly for censorship so that "immoral
and pornographic plays may be kept from polluting the youth
of the country."[21] Again, when he wrote of the literature of the
past, he lauded the thrillers of his boyhood as opposed to contemporary cheap literature, for the latter had fallen off in moral

tone. Nor were the journals and newspapers that now largely shared the responsibility for providing reading much better.

If literature should teach, McArthur was also certain that it should entertain. In belles-lettres he looked for some lightness of touch, some flash of humor. At one time, he had even contemplated a book on the Amityville philosophy, which would "be leavened of course with humour." Fiction set him a greater challenge. Aware of what and whom he disliked, he was not sure of what and whom he liked. As one would expect, the moderns displeased McArthur. The best sellers were depressing. Leacock had asserted in *Moonbeams from the Larger Lunacy* that the modern novel had abandoned storytelling to "convey a message" or "paint a picture," "or remove a veil, or open a new chapter in human psychology." McArthur agreed, except that unfortunately some of the novels tried to do all at once. Besides, none that he had read were "half as interesting as the blurbs" made them out to be.

Obviously McArthur's professed belief in progress did not apply to literature. The old masters were best. In departing from their mode, contemporary authors had gone wrong, and he looked on Tolstoi, Ibsen, and Howells as among the greatest sinners. It was they who degraded literature and so corrupted the reader, thus removing much of its *raison d'être*. Thus had McArthur allowed "Victorian morality" to influence his literary judgment. The realists neither taught nor entertained. "Only a touch of literary gloom," he writes of Leacock's *Sunshine Sketches of a Little Town*, "would be needed to make this picture of contemporary life as sordid and mean and futile as any found in the most depressing 'best seller.' "[22]

The popular Edwardians, McArthur contended, were little better. They aimed only to please. They wrote by recipe. Their fictional landscape always pictures "stately homes" and their plots always revolved about "gravel walks on which wheels can be heard or the footsteps of the hero just as the villain is about to do his worst—by request," or about the lodge "where dwells the pretty daughter who has entangled the affections of the son and heir." This type of romanticism disturbed him no less than realism, for it simply drugged the mind and left "nothing that can possibly be turned to profit, that will stimulate intellectual or spiritual growth."[23] Canadian writing, always of interest to him, disturbed him also. Gilbert Parker's Hudson's Bay stories had too specialized a setting. Pioneer novels of the approved kind, in which everything ends happily and "the hero goes into the ministry in the last chapter," irked him as well, even though he disliked books that "left his feelings harrowed." The country was not old enough for historical romances either, he suggested in a review of Anison North's *The Forging of the Pikes*.[24]

At one time McArthur believed that science would lead the way to a new kind of fiction in a kind of symbiotic relationship with art, science providing the truth, for it had proven the unity of nature, and art, the symbols for expressing this truth "in the only enduring expression" science can have.[25] This new golden age of literature was the dream of the younger McArthur. It faded as he grew older, and he turned his attention to the fiction of rural Canada, which had also failed to meet his standards. It had never worked with the proper symbols. McArthur wanted a literature that raised the farmers out of the cartoonists' world, made them something other than "creations in dialect" and gave them hope of appearing in literature as other than "stupid and sometimes amusing drudges." He longed for "that new race of poets and writers and artists which Whitman foresaw...."[26]

Here, then, was a call for realism, but realism of a special sort, for "romantic-realism," or whatever tag can be put on the kind of treatment of fact that Dickens had made popular. In a fiery reply to a correspondent McArthur belabors a "contentious" man who held that there is no romance in farming "as a sordid realist—one of those practical persons who in Keats' phrase 'could clip an angel's wings.' "[27] McArthur defined romance as an attitude of mind that finds pleasure, even in twelve below zero weather, in "keeping the fires roaring. One can sit, poker in hand, before the fire and dream unutterable dreams. And for a farmer to find a new-laid egg in a horse-manger when the thermometer is 12 below is just as romantic as getting a Christmas bonus...."[28] Farming, he concluded, is just as full of romance as any other occupation.

IV Stephen Leacock

At this point Stephen Leacock comes onstage. McArthur had tried to blend fact and fancy in his essays on farm life, but it was Leacock, he proclaims, who brought the true power of literature to bear on country life. Here at last was an author who successfully fused "the keen observation of the realist with the glamour of the idealist." In Leacock's work "the sordidness of things is not made repulsive."[29] McArthur seems to have thought that *Sunshine Sketches of a Little Town* gave promise of a novel of the kind he had tried to write in *Cayuga Brook* and that he thought Canada needed. Being "one of the truest interpreters of American and Canadian life that we have had," Leacock, "by giving free play to all his powers, may," McArthur suggests, "finally win recognition as a broad and sympathetic interpreter of life as a whole."[30] Perhaps *Sunshine Sketches of a Little Town* is not a novel *manqué*. Leacock never did write a novel that fits the definition of the word as generally understood and especially as McArthur understood it. Yet McArthur may have put his finger on one of the causes of this "arrested development." At least he was perspicacious enough to recognize the threat posed to Leacock by the publishers with their eagerness to have him repeat his most popular kind of writing and by his tendency, if not willingness, to comply. Whether Leacock lacked the aptitude to become a novelist, as Malcolm Ross will have it,[31] or whether, as Robertson Davies[32] and McArthur tend to think, circumstances precluded his becoming one, McArthur saw (and foresaw) that Leacock could, and often did, become a slave to the "attractive ... inconsequent nonsense" of *Nonsense Novels* (1911).

A liking for Leacock and a reputation as humorist and writer made McArthur, so Lorne Pierce judged, an ideal biographer-critic of Leacock, and accordingly he called on him as "the critic best qualified" and the one "who might be called the inevitable author" of a book on Leacock.[33] It was to fit the regular format of the series "The Makers of Canadian Literature"—2,500 words for biography, 10,000 for interpretation, and 16,000 for selections from the author.

From the start, then, McArthur had no leeway in the biography for tacking and hauling sail such as he had had in *Sir Wilfrid Laurier*. Besides, Leacock was very much alive and could speak for himself, if he would. McArthur had met Leacock only once and knew little of him personally. There were few, if any, newspaper clippings he "could pilfer." He needed help and at once dispatched a call to Leacock to that effect. A reply came immediately. Leacock was delighted. In a letter of January, 1923, he told Pierce he had a warm spot for McArthur, "who helped him bring out his first book," *Literary Lapses* (1910). Leacock wished to "do everything... to assist," he assured McArthur in a letter of January 26, 1923, offering "biographical stuff," suggestions for the anthology including a "fine letter from Roosevelt [to be] reproduced in facsimile," and thereby turned the projected book into a revealing exercise in self-criticism. His best he thought were "'MY FINANCIAL CAREER': The last chapter of SUNSHINE SKETCHES: 'A. B. and C' from LITERARY LAPSES: 'Q' from NONSENSE NOVELS. BEHIND THE BEYOND." Within a week he was back with more advice. The Roosevelt letter, "entirely written in his own hand is worth the whole of the book." His burlesque poetry must "have a place," since a poem of the genre "on the men I used to know at Toronto University ought to be of interest to a whole lot of people as it mentions so many by name. In the same way a McGill poem should be included."[34]

Should one trust the book or the author (or the school tie)? And what of that road paved with good intentions? Both queries must have plagued McArthur as he toiled at his book. As one answer he certainly and fortunately decided against the school tie and accepted only "My Financial Career" and the last chapter of *Sunshine Sketches of a Little Town* from the suggestions Leacock had made, but did give him the right to the last word. "The ms. will be forwarded to you for consideration," he wrote. "Anything you disapprove of will be cut out—or the whole thing will be scrapped if you don't like it."[35] McArthur answered the second query with two missives all hot from Ekrid so as to indicate that Leacock had led him some distance down the road of good intentions. One, dated May 1, threatening to "throw the whole thing up," went to Lorne Pierce since Leacock had failed to keep his promise, and another went off on May 25 to the procrastinating Leacock himself. It read somewhat testily:

Can you let me have a copy of the Roosevelt letter by return mail? I mean a typewritten copy. I want to fit it into the book and to decide whether to use it in the biography or the critical essay. As I did not hear from you any further about biographical material I went into the Morgue of the Globe and dug up the material that will be used to write your obituary. Among other things I got your contribution to Canada, 12 years ago, in which you gave the story of your life up to that date. With that to build on I have done your biography and you need not trouble sending me anything else unless there is something you particularly want mentioned.

Still that letter from Roosevelt was not forthcoming. Pierce recommended a telegram "Rush" or, if that proved ineffective, "one might," he advised, "broadcast a few of Charlie Chaplin's pies."[36] The truth is Leacock could not find the precious letter nor could William, a janitor at McGill, even with a five-dollar reward urging him to action, ferret it out. So, minus the glory of a facsimile of a letter from "Big-stick" Theodore Roosevelt "in his own hand," McArthur's study appeared, but even that lacuna did not dampen Leacock's enthusiasm. He immediately scribbled a letter to McArthur. "First rate. Fine. Excellent... too flattering, but I don't object at all."[37] McArthur himself thought "pretty well" of the book. When first approached by Pierce in January he had planned to write it in a month, since his experience, he informed Pierce, had been "that what I do hurriedly is usually much more readable than what I labour over."[38] Actually he took five months, and it may well be that many of the merits of the study derive indirectly from Leacock's tardiness, the longer period of cogitation it permitted McArthur contributing much to its organization and perceptiveness, if the hastily written *Sir Wilfrid Laurier* is a yardstick.

As critic McArthur concerned himself with character and sometimes also with the author as he revealed himself through his work. He looked on a novel as a form of biography or history and judged it on the basis of verisimilitude of characterization and validity of social comment. In "Greater Toronto," a review of Marjory MacMurchy's *The Child's House*, he adds the heroine,

Vanessa Brown, to the Toronto census. She is "one of the permanent inhabitants" of Toronto for "she lives in a book about
[the city]."[39] The great fiction of the past impressed him in the
same way. "Elia, Pendennis, Pickwick, Nigel, Oliphant and a
thousand others" were forever with him. *The Forging of the
Pikes* he esteemed highly, mostly for North's knowledge of the
uprising of 1837 and especially for its meaning in a modern
context. The tendency to focus his attention on the author comes
out most clearly when McArthur discusses literature at large,
as in his commentaries on Lanigan, Shanly, and Carman, and
this bias clearly marks his study of Leacock, but here he neatly
combines his interest in the author with an analysis of his work.
Undoubtedly something of this biographical approach to literature stems from the mode of criticism of the time, as does his
concern with character, but for McArthur interest in an artist
rather than in art seems to have come readily, a manifestation
of his broad as opposed to a "thin" and more intellectualized
humanism, and he says explicitly that he prepared his book on
Leacock after "a careful reading of his works with a view to
discovering the man back of them, . . ." "back of the fun and
fooling."[40]

Actually McArthur found several Leacocks: the humorist, the
historian, the economist, all, however, united under the banner
of "intellectual fairness." Leacock knows "what he is writing
about"; he studies "things as they are"; his burlesques are sound
at the center; he is a man of great human sympathy; he reveals
"the shams of the world, but his mockery does not tilt at the
innocent. If they blunder into laughable foolishness, the pathos
of their simplicity is not overlooked." McArthur wants to save
Leacock from those who, like his publisher, value him mainly
as humorist and that "as a frivolous entertainer," whose "wit
and antic nimbleness . . . turn life's hypocrisies to laughter."
"Surely," he continues, "it is excusable if he has his moments of
cynicism and bitterness. The more he is acclaimed for his humour
the more he must feel the futility of things."[41]

In the particular search for the man behind Leacock *the
humorist*, McArthur found not one Leacock but two, one a
boy " 'concealed behind the arras [not] feasting with the doge,' "
a youthful fun-maker and McArthur's favorite, and another, "a

man with a competent chuckle," who tends too readily to indulge in a kind of buffoonery or "lapses into humour for sophisticated grown-ups."[42] As regards motives for this ambivalence, McArthur sets forth two, stating one plainly and implying the other. The young Leacock, "exquisitely sensitive" and "shy and awkward" in the grown-up world, wrote in self-defense to stand well with "people of his own age." In the older Leacock the boy appears now only in flashes amid satire "of indignant scorn," even of "something like peevishness" and the guffaws of further foolishness. Incensed that the people do not take him seriously, Leacock, once "the aggrieved boy" of "My Financial Career" who makes youthful fun of banks, becomes at times an aggrieved man, his power of fun-making impaired, striking without mirth at the foibles of his time; or a master of revels where would-be boisterous nonsense and burlesque take preeminence and make life a farce.

The older humorist, McArthur sees in part as a victim of "modern enterprising" publishers, for they, he believes, have tempted Leacock to keep the road to popularity and success that he had taken in *Nonsense Novels* early in his literary career. Robertson Davies and Donald Cameron generally accept McArthur's thesis of Leacock the "aggrieved boy" protecting himself behind a mask of humor."[43] As yet, however, biographers, satisfied with Leacock's public image generally, have done little more than touch on Leacock the man (and certainly McArthur in his opening sketch never tries to go beyond the surface), but at that they seem to suggest an inner Leacock much as McArthur had pictured him from his reading of Leacock's books.

Much as McArthur stressed the man behind the humor, he did, though, analyze the humor perceptively. He did not argue from some critical theory and, aside from quoting critics, says nothing of it in such terms. He simply selects pathos as the foundation of Leacock's finest humor, since pathos, juxtaposed with the comic, gives it breadth and depth, enabling his humor to play on both the emotions and the intellect. The comic with pathos takes on heart and borders on tragedy, as Peter Spillikins of *Arcadian Adventures with the Idle Rich* demonstrates. Pathos, without the comic, in its turn can lead to the literary gloom of characteristic contemporary literature. *Sunshine*

Sketches of a Little Town is "very satisfying" because it fuses
the two elements. It is "very satisfying" also because it centers
in character and "such as you would find in any small town."
Thus it impresses McArthur on two counts.

"My Financial Career" likewise ranks high because it reveals
the character of youth, always an attraction for the older Mc-
Arthur. He praises Leacock here also for his use of character
"to be merry with a bank." McArthur does not concern himself
like either Ralph Curry or R. E. Watters over the nationality
of the young man. He stresses Leacock's skill in employing
irrepressible youth to poke fun at institutionalized society. As to
the true merit of *Sunshine Sketches of a Little Town,* McArthur
rests his case for its greatness with posterity; as regards his
other favorite, "My Financial Career," he is more confident, for
Leacock is "youth making laughter for youth, and the laughter
will continue while the young are shy and awkward and sensitive."[44] Unquestionably McArthur saw no irony here, unaware
that the young might not always be shy and awkward and that
neither banks nor the establishment would overawe them. He
never dreamed that urban youth might not appreciate the
"youthful Leacock" and might simply find the stories of his
bashful young people—in banks, as lovers, as guests—silly, nor
that they might think a situation far from funny in which a
young man, like Peter Pupkin, cannot marry because the bank
in which he works pays him a pittance.

Although generally Mr. McArthur, humorist, was not writing
for the delight of Leacock, humorist, the following passage
seems to have been part of the first draft of McArthur's study:

The only place where Leacock's humour seemed to fail him is in
England.

In that mysterious way in which things happen among "the best
people" the word got around that "Dear Mr. Leacock is so amusing." Then it was entirely good form to laugh and how the socially
well-disciplined people did laugh. You simply couldn't hold back if
you tried. Bishops laughed until they shook their gaiters. Heavy-
browed editors who should have been in their studies writing
"humorous leaders" on the Entente laughed and laughed . . . the
society ladies—they just let themselves go. . . . It must have been an
awful time. And there stood our keen-witted, satirical new world

humorist—but I shouldn't say stood. He fell for it. Thus did Homer nod and the classics lose class. But let it pass. . . .

This is unkind of course.

But it is no more unkind than what Sir Owen Seaman said to him. He said "Mr. Leacock's humour is really British" and instead of throwing a brick at him Mr. Leacock actually looked pleased and put it in a preface. After that who can doubt that he is just as human as the rest of us.[45]

McArthur never published this outburst and scored a victory for good taste over bad, and criticism over sarcasm. In it he must have realized that Leacock had become a whipping boy for his own bitter memories of England. He recognized a need for objectivity if his assessment were to be judicious, if, as one humorist writing of another, he were not to transform him into McArthur when he, Leacock, was a success and McArthur *manqué* when a failure. The omission did not mean, however, that McArthur intended that Leacock, except for hints about the danger of success through formula writing, should go scot-free, and he brings out some heavy guns against Leacock's satire.

McArthur knew that he had put much of himself into his work on Leacock. The "aggrieved and sensitive" boy behind the man reflects something of McArthur. He, too, had used "Laughter and Silence" as "Sword and Shield" and, when a man, he had ecstatically welcomed home the prodigal, "the laughing boy" who had taught that "life has no greater joy / Than having lived to be once more a boy."[46] This attitude unquestionably assumed a large role in his predilection for Leacock the younger, the humorist he had published in *Truth* when he himself had been young, surely an important influence in his preferences. The same attitude seems certain to have played a large part in his criticism of Leacock the older, since he, too, often lacked the whim and fancy of his younger self.

As a writer McArthur consistently held to the romantic theme of the return to innocence, and as a critic of Leacock he accepted the same criterion. "I still find flashes of the boy. I do not want to give him up." He is "very precious" to me, he acknowledges.[47] Perhaps forgetting the romantic satirists, McArthur looked askance at satire itself. It was overrated and probably did little, if any, good. (For all that, he regrets Leacock's fail-

ure to lambaste the "modern enterprising publisher.") Leacock's
satire, he argued, failed because it could not avoid slipping into
"joyous irrelevant nonsense . . . or wrath," because it tended to
stifle the elemental pathos that characterizes his best work. He
lacked the "cold ferocity" of the masters of the art and makes the
mistake of attacking "great offenders" with a "bauble" instead
of "an axe."[48] Thus spake McArthur on satire—*ex cathedra* judgments on the nature and function of satire, apparently based on
Juvenalian rather than Horatian standards. They may bring his
assessment of Leacock as satirist into question, but they leave
no doubt that he thought Leacock as satirist had taken the wrong
direction in his development.

Although McArthur undeniably discounted Leacock's satire
through personal preference and sentimental bias, he struggled
to follow the way to objectivity, to analyze, not simply to describe, his reactions to it. Besides, he stayed close to his subject,
except for one obvious break. Then he used Leacock's publishers
as the excuse for lashing out at "the curse of modern literature . . . the enterprising publisher," who, "if one book succeeds
. . . tries to lure or bulldoze the author, and every other author
over whom he has influence, to write another book like it that
will be a sure winner."[49] Coupled with contempt for forces
creating best-seller fiction was an intense scorn of the dust
jacket. For McArthur it was newfangled, hence almost axiomatically an abomination, the symbol of the deceit of modern
commercialism. Indeed, he foresaw the day when some publisher would reissue the Bible in a lurid jacket like a "best
seller."

McArthur had scarcely anything to say of Leacock the social
scientist, though he considered *The Unsolved Riddle of Social
Justice* one of the most significant in any study of Leacock. He
quoted from it once very briefly but included no selection from
it in the anthology section of his study. He tended, in fact,
"to put by his serious work" and to confine his essay to Leacock's "popular successes,"[50] a strange position in the light of
his derisive comments on those who knew, and seemed only to
want to know, the "popular" Leacock. More singular and more
commendable is the "failure" of McArthur to hold forth on his
favorite topic of social justice. That he would have thought the

book important is a foregone conclusion, that he used it so little for observations of his own certainly is not.

How his eyes must have shone when he came across such apothegms as these: "The life of a pioneer settler in America . . . stands out brightly beside the dull and meaningless toil of his descendants"; "The one thing that is wrong with socialism is that it won't work"; "Socialism is another word for slavery"; "the unspeakable savagery of Bolshevism"; "Democracy, let us grant it, is the best system of government as yet operative in this world of sin." All these points of view were attractive to McArthur, but there was another of a more general nature. McArthur recognized in Leacock's social solution (some form of welfare state) a pleasing compromise between past and present. He realized that as a Liberal, trying to reconcile his political views with an inherent conservatism, he differed little from Leacock, a conservative at heart, trying to adjust to the new demands of a postwar world. What each wished to retain was, in general terms, remarkably similar, the standards of the semipioneer period in which they had passed their childhood and youth. Here the "Red Tory" and "Blue Grit" stood on common ground.

CHAPTER 5

Essayist

I Making a Name

MᶜARTHUR began his literary career as an essayist and
gave it over only on the last day of his life, dictating his
final piece from his deathbed. Again, as he began it with
"country stuff," so he concluded it, with a description of a day
in autumn. The first essay, written when McArthur was a boy,
won him high praise from a farmer to whom he had shown it
and, he admitted years later, inspired him to try to become a
writer. One of the earliest indications that this was to be his
goal was a plan for a series of articles for the *Age* of Strathroy
that would "touch on almost all the different work or rather
phases of farm life such as: Logging bees, paring bees, barn-
raising, etc."[1] "Thrashing" and "Coon Hunting" were good, according to McKellar, and "200% better" than the short story
McArthur had submitted to *Saturday Night* at the time (1887).

McArthur soon abandoned his grand plan and in the years
that immediately followed became jokesmith, journalist, poet,
dramatist, and editor. Discovering that the essay was his forte he
turned to it in *To Be Taken With Salt: Being an Essay on Teaching One's Grandmother to Suck Eggs* (1903), his first book in
prose. Indeed, so eager was he to keep his hand in as essayist
that when his work as advertising manager of W. T. Stead's
paper precluded his writing, he proposed to his American friend
Vaux that they discuss various topics in their letters, which they
could collect as a book. McArthur wished, he said, to lay aside
the cap and bells, and to prove his point drew up as a starter
this sobersided list of phenomenological teasers—science, consciousness, immortality, time, space, and motion. He managed
the first three, and then the project collapsed. He liked chatting
too much to keep to such metaphysical heights. A book at the

expense of that congenial pastime was too high a price to pay.

Keep his hand in he did, however, and when he finally laid his pen aside he had published hundreds of essays: eight in *Punch* (1902–03); 1,214 in the *Globe,* Toronto (May 29, 1909, to November 1, 1924)—a few were short pieces, "Cartoons in Words" and "Farm Fables"; 299 in the *Farmer's Advocate* (February 3, 1910 to February 2, 1922); not to mention others (some anonymous) in publications such as the *Atlantic Monthly,* the *Journal of Commerce,* the *Forum,* the *Farmer's Magazine,* the New York *Sun,* and the several pamphlets about insurance he produced in the last years of his life. His books *In Pastures Green* (1915), *The Red Cow and Her Friends* (1919), *The Affable Stranger* (1920), and *Around Home* (1925) are compilations he himself made from his *Globe* and *Farmer's Advocate* columns, and *Familiar Fields* (1925) and *Friendly Acres* (1927) contain essays from the earlier collections and other favorites selected by McArthur's son Daniel. Kenneth Wells in his edition of *In Pastures Green* (1949) presumptuously removed all references to politics and economics "since Peter would have realized" that they "are black and arid blots in a green field."[2] *The Best of Peter McArthur* (1968), edited by A. Lucas, attempts to be both representative and selective of McArthur's work and contains many essays not previously published in book form.

McArthur proposed to collect his political satires, but his plans came to nought, and his remarks on his failure tell a sad story, not so much because the book never appeared but because of what it discloses of the state and nature of Canadian publishing in the early 1920's, for he found that by July (1923) Canadian publishers had already decided to publish no more Canadian books that year. If, however, some company in the United States would take his book, then at least one of the Canadian houses promised to buy a Canadian edition.

Unfortunately McArthur never succeeded in matching his income with his industry, except when editing *Truth.* During the years he wrote for the *Globe* and the *Farmer's Advocate,* he earned no princely sum. At first he received ten dollars a week from each, but in 1914 they increased their payments to fifteen dollars. Occasionally he picked up a bit extra—a series of thirty articles on apples for three hundred fifty dollars, lecture tours that netted four to five hundred dollars in a year—but he can hardly be said to have made writing a financial success. Late in 1912 he joined a writer's syndicate, but by early 1914 he was his own man again, withdrawing from it when he recognized that all the great scheme had ever meant was a longer wait for his *Globe* stipend. If he made no money, he lost none either, since the syndicate started as it ended, "a combintion of writers without capital."[3]

As for the books, they sold enough for prestige but did not bring in much money he told Vaux. *In Pastures Green* went through two editions of two thousand each fairly quickly, selling at $2.50 a book. *The Red Cow and Her Friends* was not so popular, and five hundred copies of the first edition, along with the few second edition remainders of *In Pastures Green,* were finally bought by the government of Manitoba for use in the provincial public school libraries. *The Affable Stranger,* which received many laudatory reviews, sold poorly and may well have been one of the reasons Thomas Allen shied away from an advance of five hundred dollars against royalties for McArthur's book of political satires. *The Last Law—Brotherhood* (1921), his last collection of essays, netted him fifteen hundred dollars as a flat fee.

Although McArthur never achieved his dream of writing a best seller, he would have if the public had been willing to buy books they had previously read in the newspapers, for he was an extremely popular columnist during the early decades of this century. It was a time when rural Canada was moving from the age of the horse and buggy to that of the automobile, and McArthur, alive to the purport of the transition, became its chief interpreter. Many of the city people, migrants from the farms, could, through his articles, take a sentimental journey to their old homes again and to their youth, a not insignificant element in their appreciation of McArthur's work. Others, city-bred, could dream of the quiet life if they could not relive it in memories. As for the farmers, they were wakened to a world they had never known before, though they had been born into it.

City and country alike also could enjoy the hijinks of McArthur's horse, Dolly, a temperamental driver, and the peccadilloes of the Red Cow, Fenceviewer I, and her equally capricious daughter, Fenceviewer II, not overlooking of course the august presence of the old gobbler, or the belligerencies of the titled goat, Sir Clifford Sifton, and the old warrior, Socrates, the ram, in a rural drama that had a run of sixteen years without losing its hold on the public. Here McArthur was following the technique of the continued story with episodes in which the same characters continued to appear and also with his animal name tags to facilitate characterization and to aid reader recall. Again, the vogue of the animal story in the early nineteenth century may have had some bearing on his success, but certainly there was no Black Beauty or Beautiful Joe on the farm at Ekfrid. McArthur fought no battles for the rights of animals by creating make-believe beasts; he simply described those that he kept on his farm.

McArthur had other strings to his bow and between acts of his animal dramas took time to talk about farming, nature, and the philosophy of the simple life, to explain and argue about contemporary politics and economics, urbanization, specialization, and other problems relating to the rural community. He kept free, however, of matters pertaining to sex and organized religion, through either personal predilection or from deference to a public close-lipped about the one and close-minded about the other. Despite these lacunae, or perhaps because of them, his appeal was widespread, as this record of his correspondence for a single week indicates, with such people writing to him as a judge, a lawyer, a Member of Parliament, the Deputy Minister of Marine, an astronomer, a weather prophet, a hired man, a maker of artificial limbs, three farmers, and a young lady.[4] In this comment McArthur touches on another and related reason for his popularity, namely, the opportunity he gave his readers to participate in his work. He sometimes asked questions and published the answers he received. In this way he kept a finger on the public pulse and could judge his work accordingly.

The authenticity of the material, the sense of reality that pervaded it, also helped make McArthur's work attractive. Familiarity, McArthur argued, does not rob things of their wonder, and he held that "the one hit [he] made with the public he made by giving the small details of farm life."[5] Emile Jones, the heroine of *Cayuga Brook*, McArthur's unpublished novel, lamented that it must be easier to write of Rome or "some old romantic place" than a land like Canada, where "our everyday lives are so commonplace. Moreover even when Canadian writers set their books here," she continues, "they often make it seem as if it were not Canada they were writing about at all." At this juncture Mrs. Jones, resenting the complaint, gently admonishes Emile. " 'Yes, my dear ... but you must remember that they are geniuses.' "[6]

McArthur made sure that he would never belong with any of the authors Emile may have had in mind, for he set out to convince Canadians that he was writing about Canada, and actually he was producing for the first time in Canada the kind of literature about rural life that gave, and he thought should give, on the authority, too, of his revered Thoreau, " 'a romantic glamour to country life [so that] culture, instead of being handed down from the heights, will be handed up, or rather we shall have to go back to the soil to get it.' "[7] McArthur knew how to make the most of the commonplace. "At all times," he says, "I told the truth, merely garnishing it with humour, poetry, and philosophy."[8] Whether McArthur is a romantic realist or a realistic romantic, the romantic does not deny a seriousness of subject. All search for a form to behave in. McArthur discovered one for himself and finding it good prescribed it for others. It is no mere chance that the first sentence in *In Pastures Green,* his first book of his series about country living, reads, "We are a hopelessly unromantic people."

Almost all McArthur's essays are personal and, like good essays of the kind, gain much from the character of their author, for McArthur leaves an overriding impression not only of geniality but of such knowledge and common sense that in his own day his readers dubbed him "the sage of Ekfrid" (a title he disliked since he thought it made him seem old). McArthur was never bland or cute or clever. He could be nostalgic, disputatious, sarcastic, but most of all he was a warmhearted man with a fine sense of humor. Well-informed and alert-minded, he applied himself to the task of propounding the philosophy of the simple life, and as he seldom tried to be humorous for the sake of being funny, neither did he play with ideas for the sake of being smart nor sneer at practical common sense as unintellectual. If a local colorist, McArthur is a man whose experiences in the urban world gave his work a breadth and depth beyond the parochial.

Comprehending both geniality and intelligence was the imaginative sympathy McArthur had with his subject. In advising Daniel of the art of writing he set out these points: "Don't write anything as a stunt . . . think deeply and sympathetically . . . express yourself with sincerity."[9] McArthur knew how to be serious without being dull, humorous without being a buffoon, how to be an intellectual without losing himself in the clouds, or, as the *Globe* has it, there was "something akin to genius" about the man.

The attractiveness of many of the essays depends on the "romantic glamour" that derives from McArthur's discovery that even if you can go home again, you can't go back to youth again. Frequently whole essays like "Whittlin'" and "My Friends, the Trees" are *ubi sunt* in mood. More often the wistfulness is indicated only momentarily, but perhaps even more poignantly because of its brevity, as in this aside: "Of all who were in the crowd going to the fair I envied the boys the most, and wished that I could see things they were looking at with the same wonder and unspoiled enthusiasm they felt."[10] The "romantic glamour" of the essays derives also from descriptions of living close to nature—"boiling in" maple sap when spring with its renewed life surges out of winter, tending garden when the world seems a "June Reverie," harvesting crop lands drowsy in the summer sun, searching for mushrooms in early autumn mornings, or reading in a cozy room as the cold settles over the countryside under a high, bright, winter moon.

Sometimes to add information to an essay or to defend some point McArthur drew on authority, looking up "profound references in the encyclopaedias and other deep works with which the house is cluttered,"[11] but the essays leave the impression generally that he got along on his own. Not so, however, when he wished to stress the imaginative or the poetic (for him synonymous with the romantic) quality of his material, for then he quoted without restraint so that the quotation and the literary allusion are as distinctive a characteristic of his work as his humorous touches. According to one report, McArthur "could repeat page after page, without a pause, of a volume that particularly interested him,"[12] and he never hesitated to dip into this capital. "Proverbs and quotations," says a manuscript note, "constitute the real racial literature that bears the imprint of the oversoul. Only what is easily quotable of any author's work belongs to real literature. The rest of his work is vanity and vexation of spirit."[13]

So much for theory; on a more practical level McArthur confesses "a weakness for quotations," but, instead of looking on them "as ornaments," regards them as "first aids to expression—an easy way to get out of hammering out phrases and sentences to express ideas. . . . Why dress your ideas in 'hodden gray' when you can borrow from 'silken Samarcand'? I know there are honest people who take their quotations seriously and wear them only on State occasions, but I have never been able to acquire the necessary dignity. When in need I reach for the first quotation that comes handy, even though the result may be as incongruous as 'a precious jewel in an Ethiop's ear.' "[14]

Some of this at least must be taken with a grain of salt, for an examination of over one hundred quotations discloses greater care in selecting them than McArthur implies here, for they fall into patterns. First and most commonly they function as illustrative material, enhancing the thought or mood of the commentary. They are often taken out of context, or "misapplied," to put it in another way, and give a kind of literary dimension to the nonliterary. Yelling in the sugar bush brings to mind lines from *The Song of Roland*: "A blast of that dread horn / On Fontarabian echoes borne."[15] "Stevenson," he says, "probably had woodchucks in mind when he wrote

'They lay in a blessed swound
For days and days together
In their dwellings underground.' "[16]

Here the light touch intends no parody, but in several instances McArthur resorts to it openly for the sake of humor or to reinforce his social criticism. Shakespeare helps him protest the hard work of planting trees, for he fears lest

" 'This great sea of jobs rushing upon me
O'erbear the shore of my mortality,
And drown me with their sweetness.' "[17]

Tennyson appears in this modernized version, "The individual withers, and the company is more and more."[18]

For all that McArthur's essays are filled with literally hundreds of quotations and literary allusions, few of which are from Canadian writers, there is nothing pedantic about his use of them, not even those that he has "taken seriously." He simply had the knack of quoting pertinently. Still, references to the classics, the old masters, and the philosophers may seem out of place for rural audiences. Deacon suggests that he was trying to help the farmer attain a "more satisfactory attitude toward life . . . to induce him to take broader views."[19] This assessment is of course in keeping, up to a point, with McArthur's aim to preach the simple life, but there is more to it than the didactic. It reveals McArthur's deep-seated love of literature and learning and his attempts to fuse the sophisticated and the rustic in his art and philosophy. The primitive was not enough. One needed the great artists as interpreters. He wanted to be an academic, yet not a academic; a farmer, yet not a farmer. He was not aiming solely at giving the farmer an education and a taste of culture. He was also keeping alive within himself as a writer and man something of an attitude from the past when literature meant all in all to him. Perhaps he did believe that it was an adjunct to nature, but, writing for such an audience as he had, he feared the smell of the lamp and had little choice but to make it secondary.

Frequently McArthur's idealism produced not only essays devoted to the "romantic glamour" of country life, but to criticism, often harsh, of those, farmer and urbanite alike, who were blind to it and would subvert it. Here again he becomes the satirist and social critic he had been in the days when he wrote for *Punch* and published *To Be Taken With Salt*. McArthur had still another method by which he attempted to teach and delight his audience, for much that he wrote revealed a twinkle in his eye. Indeed, his humor permeates so much of his prose that one library filed all his articles—on nature, on farm life, and on public affairs—under humor, recognizing prophetically, it now seems, the quality of his work that for many has worn best. Deacon held that McArthur's farm humor would not last since the changing conditions of farm life would make it unintelligible.[20] Yet in two recent anthologies, *Great Canadian Writing: A Century of Imagination* (edited by Claude Bissell, 1966) and *A Treasury of Canadian Humour* (edited by Robert Allen, 1967), McArthur won a place precisely because of it.

II *The Art of the* Causerie

As essayist McArthur has been likened to Montaigne, since both raised the ordinary to "a place of enduring charm."[21] Other critics have found similarities between his work and Eugene Field's and David Grayson's. Whatever these parallels may be, McArthur was really on his own. The subject was his and, for the most part, the form, too, since he most frequently used the *causerie* or chat, rather than the formal essay, as a way of expression, although, "Reciprocity," "Why I Stick to the Farm," and many others—each with its central topic and theme and unified structure of introduction, discussion, and conclusion—prove his ability with the genre.

The *causerie,* an almost formless form of literary expression, depends almost entirely on the author's ability as a conversationalist for its ultimate success. It suited McArthur admirably, for he was a good conversationalist and, moreover, could move from the spoken word to the written without losing ground. It gave him the freedom, also, to treat several different matters in one commentary, to satisfy his desire to cover a wide area related to farm life at any one time, and to discuss concerns of the moment at the moment. The reader of McArthur's rural "diary," *In Pastures Green,* finds that on May 3 it offers a fine spread of no fewer than six topics—small farms, road building, public-spirited men, spring weather, wintering bees, and brooding hens.

Through the *causerie,* also, he had an almost endless combination of modes that he could employ to give variety to his work. He narrates or dramatizes events. He describes scenes and activities. He draws character sketches, presents vignettes, and writes apostrophes. The *causerie* opened the door to the kind of casualness and spontaneity he wished to establish with his readers. Some of this attitude may have derived from his wish to defend work that he had to do quickly, and hence often sloppily, in order to maintain his newspaper commitments and farm pursuits simultaneously. Yet he was in a dilemma. He wanted his work to appear as natural as a chat over a roadside fence so as to be acceptable to the farmers, and he even resorts to belittling his *Globe* and *Farmer's Advocate* columns as "airy persiflage" and "nonsense." This kind of comment seems, nevertheless, as much a defense against criticism as an effort to establish himself as "genial host." McArthur, as his letters to Vaux disclose, suffered doubts about his "country stuff" and in moments of self-depreciation tried to make amends by a public confession that demonstrated, like his quotations, his awareness of other literary standards. Like his humor and satire, his disavowal of his "country stuff" gave him a chance to hide.

Despite frequent (and often a more apparent than real) lack of unity, McArthur's *causeries* are not as the critic Kenneth Wells, blinded by a flash of his own wit, describes them. Following McArthur, he complains, was "like following a furrow drawn by a cider-filled farm hand at midnight behind a runaway horse."[22] For one thing, as already noted, McArthur often wrote of more than one subject and in more than one mode in a single entry in *In Pastures Green* or in his newspaper articles, but each section was complete in itself, and often all sections were united by tone, attitude, or atmosphere. Time also serves to unify his discussions—linear time to present a day on the farm, to relate present to past, to unify a whole book in terms of nature's annual cycle, and simultaneous time for aspects of an incident, say, a storm, and for his seasonal landscapes and rural panoramas.

Another of McArthur's favorite devices for organizing his material was contrast or comparison. Sometimes one part of an essay becomes a balance for the other, as in a discussion of William Wordsworth, where the regularly spaced intrusion of a boy to report on farm problems serves most impressively to yoke the abstract and the actual together dialectically.[23] More often one part of an essay comments on the other, as in "Snow Stuff," and "Mushrooms and Rain" even goes so far as to make the second half a burlesque of the first. Often these contrasts and comparisons operate on several levels, as "The Carefree Woodchuck" exemplifies, where summer and winter, inner and outer, man and animal are the elements that give the "character sketch" both its unity and its tension. Occasionally, to cite "Educate Him" and "Fishin'" as only two examples, he dramatizes a situation or describes it, coming upstage now and then to analyze or comment on some phase of it.

McArthur often digresses on the basis of the free association of ideas. As with authorial intrusion in fiction, it can be argued, however, that there is nothing inherently wrong about his practice if it adds interest to a discussion or significant overtones hinting at a new context for an essay. Besides, he normally comes back either explicitly or implicitly to round out his discussion via linkages. "But to return," "That reminds me that," and similar expressions pop up here and there, and once he adopted a kind of refrain, "How's that," to keep things together. He hardly ever uses an introduction. He may hint at what is to come ("I should have known better"), make a statement, or ask a rhetorical question, preferring to organize his material deductively for the most part. Similarly, his conclusions are concise, pertinent, and rarely moralizing. He describes setting a sheep's broken leg and then suddenly brings all to a head in a light assessment of the whole affair. "By the way, I wonder if they give prizes for animal bonesetting at the Fall Fairs. I must find out."[24]

Even when he recognizes his failure to "keep to his subject," he tries to save the day with some comment like: "But this is wandering far from the garden and the lettuce bed—all of which goes to show that you can raise ... things besides vegetables in a garden."[25] Such an observation may not do much for structure, but it is in keeping with the personality of the man chatting. Even at the conclusion of essays that seem peevish, McArthur is often able to reestablish his affability. "Now that I have rid myself of the curse of work for this spring," he writes, "and have scolded about it for a page or so I shall begin to look into important matters like [tree-toads' croaking]...."[26] Of course these illustrations demonstrate the most important unifying force of all, namely, McArthur's personality, for it is stamped indelibly on all his country stuff.

In the first flush of success in Canada, McArthur found that the universities and normal schools endorsed his homely articles as models of composition and one examinee even honored him as " 'one of the great writers of the Victorian era.' "[27] Not so later critics Deacon, Wells, and Conron. Says Deacon, McArthur's style became sloppy in later years; says Wells, "McArthur's style is loose and hurried"; and Conron supports them, refusing to excuse McArthur's "carelessness" on the basis of "homely charm."[28]

Undoubtedly much of McArthur's later prose lacks polish and undoubtedly much—not "all," as Conron claims—is "rambling, loose, and colloquial,"[29] characteristics, by the by, that do not damn it out of hand. Moreover, there are two McArthur prose styles, one of the early years when he was writing for *Truth* and *Punch* and a later one that characterizes a good number of the farm essays. In those early days he was fastidious and read books on style and wrote and rewrote much of *To Be Taken With Salt* several times. He had no time for such luxury when the *Globe* and the *Farmer's Advocate* were forever at his heels, and, as much work can mean much bad work, his prose suffered accordingly. Moreover, in an effort to be chatty, he became very informal. Far too many sentences begin with conjunctions and wander through various constructions before they conclude. Paragraphs become unduly discursive. More damning, however, is diction.

At times McArthur, who "is strong for holidays," is "all fussed up" over a "bunch of work." Occasionally his taste fails him, and he inserts an outlandishly colloquial sentence in the midst of a fine discourse, and the whole piece crashes. "As the stars were blotted out by the light, all except the larger ones and a planet that hung in the west like a drop of liquid silver, the snow began to light up with infinite constellations. There was moonlight and snow 'Fur's you cud look or listen.' "[30] He becomes wordy, repetitious, and awkward and ought to have rewritten passages such as this when he published his columns as books.

The progress of Strafe, the lamb that had his leg broken, is about the most surprising that I have seen in a long time. One naturally thinks of a broken leg as a serious thing, and it is to a human being, but it doesn't seem to cause so very much discomfort to a lamb.... Of course he was hampered by his game leg, which was bound up in the splints I had put on it, but he found little difficulty in climbing to the top of a pile of hay that had been thrown from the top of a stack and defending his position against assaulting forces.[31]

Such references show McArthur at his worst, for he can write excellent prose. His diction is simple; his nouns are concrete; his verbs, lively. Though not given to adjectives and figures of speech, he can create vivid similes and apt and imaginative phrases. "The mercury was sulking at zero." "A door bulged open." "Horseradish is robustiously countrified. Its vitamines are on tiptoe all the time." There are dozens of expressions of the kind in his essays and occasionally one of more flamboyant imagery shows up, to call to witness the angry man who "let the big bouncing adjectives roll down from the sulphur-blue heights of his eloquence."[32] McArthur can also write a clean-cut expository prose, that most difficult of all forms, as "Fresh Fish," which instructs the reader how to fillet fish, demonstrates. At the other end of the register he can write remarkably sensuous descriptive prose without resorting to purple passages or mere word painting.

After some days of this teasing, a storm came that somehow could not slip off to the north or to the south. It came at us squarely with a front like Niagara and a great rushing wind before it. It crackled with thunder and blazed with lightning, and the first downpour was mingled with hail. It lasted for only a few minutes, but while it lasted it was a veritable cloud-burst. The spouting eaves could not carry all their treasures, but overflowed in splashing and tinkling rivulets. And the murmur we heard was not all of the falling rain. It was full of the thanksgiving of the grass and of the leaves that were held up like cupped palms to catch the reviving shower. When the cloud passed and the sun came out a great sigh of relief seemed to go up from all nature and once more the music of the birds was grateful and sweet to hear.[33]

McArthur's essays are unique in Canadian literature. They are inspired by a love of the farming world, yet they say little of community interests, except as they relate to the pioneers. They seldom discuss people, and then usually only in passing refer-ences to members of the family or to that great generality, the

Big Businessman. They tell of the land and the life that it makes possible, on one level an original contribution—Conron calls it a pastoral—to Canadian literature and on another a convincing espousal of Canadian nationhood.

CHAPTER 6

Humorist

I Jokesmith and Satirist

M cARTHUR theorized little about humor. A manuscript note comments that it is "based on deviations from laws and the incongruity that results. . . . The man who deviates from the law of gravitation provokes mirth but no more than he who deviates from that other law of nature called love."[1] This remark does not, however, explain all, for McArthur divided humor into two categories: "cheerful humor" and satire. By "cheerful humor" he meant comic eccentricity or absurdity fused with geniality and high spirits. It aims to provoke laughter but not at its subject, for it does not make comparisons between the subject and accepted social standards in order to deride its weaknesses. Satire fitted the terms of the note. It compared its subject with standards for the sake of ridicule. McArthur did not necessarily associate it with laughter and in his later years found fault with Leacock as a satirist for being too gentle, for failing to use an ax to assault wrongdoers. He even denied the validity of satire altogether, because humor and laughter make life more endurable.[2] These are revealing remarks. They indicate how far McArthur finally went in misconstruing the nature of satire by separating it from subtlety and humor.

For the most part the value and practice of humor concerned McArthur much more than its nature and source. Smiles and jokes and laughter were more than mere "laughing matter." They brought people together "on terms of equality," for they helped remove "the seeming inequalities of life."[3] They taught people to recognize how amusing their struggles and misadventures are when seen from the outside, how much they appear like a lovers' quarrel to an understanding adult.

McArthur began his professional career as a satirist of sorts in the late 1880's in Toronto, where he earned $2.50 for a weekly page of jokes for John Wilson Bengough's magazine *Grip*, and during the early 1890's in New York, where he again lived largely on his earnings from his jokes, receiving one to three dollars each for them from *Judge, Life*, and similar magazines and knocking them off, according to W. A. Deacon, at the rate of ten an hour when in stride.[4] This feat demanded considerable wit, energy, and courage, for, according to the editor of *Life*, McArthur had "a joke output equalled only by two other practitioners of this exacting vocation; one of whom went mad and the other of whom committed suicide."[5]

Most of McArthur's jokes appeared anonymously and are of the old-fashioned dialogue sort with a straight man to set up the comparisons on which wit rests for its effects. He was fond of character jokes, where type is the general hypothesis by which this comparison is implied or stated. He liked Irish and English, but apparently not Scotch, jokes, since out of 841 examined not one was of the kind. He also wrote the bashful lover, the catty woman, and the "nigger" joke, all of which were popular at the time. Among the relatively few jokes focused on the professions, editors, poets, and clergymen, the farmer outnumbered all. Others received some attention, but strangely, in view of McArthur's later work, the farmer as country rube became a favorite subject, while the businessman, the target of almost all his satire in years to come, got off with scarcely a mention.

McArthur's jokes are for the most part mildly satiric jibes at human failings, but he employs many means to obtain humorous effect, such as chop logic, free association, and exaggeration. Frequently the humor derives entirely from verbal play—puns, ambiguities, dialect, bad grammar, bad spelling, misapplied metaphors and similes. McArthur knew the tricks of the trade and used them all, or nearly all. He avoided the salacious entirely in situation or language, including even the suggestive *double entendre*, though once he risked having a photographer speak of a print of a woman as being "over-exposed." Sometimes the humor was farfetched and depended on a heading, as in the following: "HE WAS UNDOUBTEDLY A POE - T, wherein Witticus proves Poe was a poet to a T." Sometimes it derived from an accompanying cartoon, very often a picture of a violent practical joke. His humor also took the form of the epigram, which normally he made into a "philosophical" witticism about life or honed to stiletto sharpness for purposes of social criticism.

After this auspicious start as jokesmith, McArthur soon branched out into light satirical verse, short stories, and tales, especially in the magazine *Truth* when he edited it, and it was not until he went to England that he took up satirical nonfiction again. Always a man of literary ambitions, he had helped his cause at the time with a letter to the editor of *Punch* informing him that a visit to Westminster Abbey had saddened him, for there is always a melancholy pleasure in contemplating the place where one expects to be buried. The editor, attracted by the wit, invited McArthur to write something he thought suitable. Even then there were signs of things to come, for the first two articles McArthur submitted were "too sarcastic to suit them" and were returned with suggestions to "be more genial," but he learned his lessons well. *Punch* accepted eight pieces within a year (1902–1903). Two of these pieces, "Canada as she is Misunderstood" and "Another 'Great Misunderstood,' " are prospectuses of histories he conjectured writing, the first on Canada's ridiculous notions about England and the second on England's ridiculous notions about Canada. Social criticism, they are written with delicate tongue-in-cheek cheekiness as in the first prospectus, where Chapter IV lampoons English ignorance with a "digression in which the author proves that when the North Pole is finally discovered it will be found somewhere in the centre of Canada."

II To Be Taken With Salt

McArthur followed his success with *Punch* with his first book, *To Be Taken With Salt: Being an Essay on Teaching One's Grandmother to Suck Eggs*, in which he reprinted his two prospectuses. Like them the book centers in social criticism, and is itself a collection of essays that hang together as satire of English ways and characteristics and in particular as the autobiography of a colonial (Peter McArthur trying to make good in London as an advertising agent) who finds that his grandmother (England) has many eggs in her basket—commerce and banking, various social classes, and many colonies—and that she knows how to get the most from each. Although the allegory of the eggs is an ingenious application of a folk expression, it adds little, however, to the satire and does not really supply a framework for the essays.

Critical in general of the British, *To Be Taken With Salt* finally demonstrates that a young man who had gone overseas full of North American "know-how" on the one hand and romantic notions of England on the other had misjudged England and largely because he had misjudged himself. He realizes eventually that he has been a dupe despite his "astuteness," and at the end of the book sets out his conclusions about his experiences, as if "to moralize his song," in a series of fifty-six epigrams that are hardly genial satire. The editor of *Punch* was no longer watchdog, and the hero seems to be taking the opportunity of getting his own back on England vicariously by word. "An Englishman's social standing," he observes, "seems to depend on the number of people he can afford to despise." City high-life came under attack, also. "London is full of clever people who expect to get salvation in a moment and spread the luxury of being damned over a life time." The acerbity here is matched in this tribute to British traditionalism, "The average Englishman has so deep a reverence for antiquity that he would rather be wrong than be recent."[6]

To focus on a Canadian in London was an original perspective for a Canadian book and an excellent device for satire, not only of the British and Americans, but of Canadians also, as the last of the epigrams illustrates: "England is the place to which prominent Canadians come clothed and in their right minds and go back wearing knee breeches and rejoicing in a title that leaves the friends of their youth in doubt whether they should be addressed as, say, Sir Jingo, Sir Mr. Jingo, or Sir Jingo McBore."[7] Then in a brilliantly ironic scene the book concludes with the hero defending the British against the criticism of an American who finds the same faults with them that the hero had, but who was not going to have anyone convert him. "Work off a British polish on Me? ON ME?" he shouts as he leaves the book, and McArthur gives his study of Old World–New World relationships another dimension. The incident, however, had its advantages for the hero. He entertained "the company at Lord Bandy-legs' that evening with a diverting account of the fellow's insolence."[8]

Much of *To Be Taken With Salt* dramatizes the themes of the epigrams. In one scene, set in a hotel, the British servant with his "Yes, sir. Thank you, sir. Thank you, sir. Yes, sir," holds center stage.[9] In another and one of the funniest in the book, the hero meets "The Lone New Zealander."

> ...my train of thought was suddenly interrupted by a man who was sitting at the opposite side of the table. He was worrying a rump steak, and showing marked symptoms of returning to a feral state.
>
> Feeling that I had to do with a case of reversion to type I resolved to humour him and began as Mowgli might when addressing one of his fellows of the jungle.
>
> "Good killing?" I enquired, unconcernedly.
>
> He dropped his knife and fork and glared at me for a moment, then shook his head, muttering, "No, no, I was mistaken; I did not hear a human voice addressed to me." He then returned with a snarl to his steak.
>
> Something of pathos about him made me persist.
>
> "Beastly weather we've been having lately," I remarked, adopting the usual British form of salutation.
>
> At this he sprang from his seat, and, leaning across the table, asked in a voice trembling with emotion, "Did you really speak to me?"
>
> "I did," I replied, relieving the embarrassment by shaking him warmly by the hand.
>
> This action on my part touched him so deeply that he burst into tears. Waiting until his emotion had somewhat spent itself, I enquired the cause of his distress.
>
> Striking a dramatic attitude, he exclaimed impressively, "I am the lone New Zealander.... Exactly three months ago I left the hemisphere of the moa and the ornithorhynchus to visit the metropolis of the world. Despite the advice and experience of my friends, I brought not a single letter of introduction."[10]

Matching the dramatized satire of the book is a diary that it contains midway through, telling of the visit of the young man to "his uncle," the pawnbroker, from whom he learns that all his trinkets are cheap American jewelry and that he is now penniless. The satire here turns inward and becomes ironical. The hero passes through a period of "romantic agony" of pride, anger, and self-pity in which McArthur ridicules the arrogance of the hero's early attitudes, when he was going to show the British. Much of the diary comprises blank pages to demonstrate in mock epic style the true center of the young man, not to mention the fun it pokes at the normal diary. What is worse, the hero admits, in his last entry, that what he has written is false. "Not even the condition I was then in could make me drop my pose and tell the absolute truth."[11] One wonders whether Mc-Arthur, in making this remark, had particularly in mind the entry in which the young romantic in a moment of self-deprecia-tion mourns his past follies. "Tonight I am heart-sick at the thought of the little kindnesses I might have shown and did not. Always I said to those whom I loved 'Wait! My golden dreams will soon come true and then you shall want for nothing.' Some of them are dead—died empty-handed and empty-hearted. Some have won for themselves and have passed out of my life—and some are poor and old and indifferent. That is what I think as the last of my dreams fades into the darkness of a London night."[12] The passage would seem to justify McArthur's remark that humor can be both sword and shield. The youthful Lea-cock was not the only one who knew the art of hiding " 'behind the arras or feasting with the doge,' " as McArthur was to say of him years later.[13]

Corresponding to the personal satire of the diary was a remarkable chapter of descriptive social satire on those who would kill time and annihilate space. This is of course an attack on the machine age, a subject that was to occupy McArthur to the end of his career. He was no cynic. He had values and, romantic as he was, he set England's failings in the modern world off against her greatness in the past—the visionary age of Eliza-beth—and in the future, too, for she could be great again if she would only set up a "Stock Exchange for dreams." As to be expected, this dealt in the values of the past and especially of those who had gone to the colonies to make new homes. Modernity had values, but wrong ones, and McArthur concludes his chapter with a dream in which a Mentor sententiously argues for idealism, advising him that time and space are but limitations of the mind. "To those who regard Time and Space as outward and real, they are real," he says, "and those who strive to destroy them, they will destroy. But to all who have raised their hope to the Infinite and Eternal, they are neither destroyers nor to be destroyed but shadows that veil the too ardent truth lest it blind our vision. . . .

"I bowed my head in reverent meditation, and behold, Time was with me again in the fulness of his youth, and Space was once more flooded with the life-giving sunlight of Heaven."[14]

Here the hero assumes the role not so much of prodigal as of penitent, but the two are closely linked and reveal much the same attitudes toward the past. As regards the satire, the long sermonizing conclusion seems out of place, but the final sentence puts all in doubt, irony being as two-edged as it is. "When I looked forth the vision had passed and I saw that as men regard it, I had killed as much Time as one usually does in reading a chapter of a somewhat frivolous book."[15] The ambiguity here is not so much satire as fear of the nakedness of print and open confession. Undoubtedly McArthur was outlining Amityville philosophy in the chapter, but while he still held to it his experiences in life made him hesitant to acknowledge it as he had once planned to in the magazine *Originator*. Satire often betrays a lack of self-confidence.

Regrettably McArthur never again tried a book like *To Be Taken With Salt*. It was a "rather strange affair," he admitted, but he had high hopes for it. Unfortunately it turned out to be a "complete frost." The warehouse in which it was kept prior to distribution burned. The publisher became bankrupt. The printer went into receivership. McArthur could, he said, "put up a defence of its apparent incoherence, but you know 'One should never spoil a good theory by explaining it.' "[16]

III *"Educate Him"*

To Be Taken With Salt was the last of its kind, but not McArthur's farewell to satire. He set himself up in his "country stuff" as a guardian of the farm world, which often required his having a sharp tongue and a heavy fist. He had no Sam Slick or other persons, however, through whom he could call the farmer to account and so normally simply made critical, authorial remarks when he wished to find fault. One could argue, also, that on the occasions when he focuses on his own failings as a farmer he intends to let farmers see themselves without his having to make any direct allusion to them. As a way of satirizing the city world, however, he did create a character, Sir Jingo McBore, whom he then lampooned in limerick and essay. A stock figure, Sir Jingo was merely a whipping boy for all McArthur's animosities toward big business and was scarcely much more than a name. He was never developed, but showed no promise of having the vitality of Sam Slick.

McArthur liked best to use satire in asides, but now and then he devoted a whole essay to lambasting some urbanite or other, as in "Educate Him." Tired of the insistence of the business world that education can cure all the farmers' ills, McArthur sends Sir Philabeg McSporran, Senator Redneck, and Mr. Gosh Whatawad to school to farmer Bill Simmons. There is nothing sly about the satire; the characters of the "students" are undifferentiated; yet there is vigor and directness about them and their speech that lifts the satirical to the humorous. The language, the imagery, "now my pretty ones," and the tone are right, even if the pedagogy is out-of-date.

"Now, my pretty ones," says Bill, "If a railroad is built under a government charter, with the assistance of the public treasury, and is then presented to the company that built it, to whom should that railroad finally belong?"

"To me," pipes Sir Philabeg, who is a High Financier and understands how to manipulate the market.

"Wrong," says our bucko from lot 17, seventh concession of Alfalfa township. "It will belong to the peepul—at least sufficiently so to justify them in regulating its operations so that it will serve the best interests of the community. You may go to your seat, Sir Philabeg, and figure it out, and I will come around with the tug in a few minutes and see that you have it right."

Then the grim instructor goes on: "What is a Big Interest?"

"A corporation that contributes liberally to our campaign fund," says Senator Redneck, with a knowing smile.

"Wrong!" booms Simmons. "The Biggest Interest in this country is farming and after that comes labour—both engaged in producing the real wealth of the country."[17]

McArthur used burlesque again (but never quite so successfully). With its close relative, the mock epic, he was more
consistently good. The aristocratic sport of fox hunting becomes,
as McArthur describes it, a story of some boys and a man
traipsing through the snow, and the native sport of "coon hunting," revered throughout the countryside, begins, when Mc-
Arthur engages in it, with Sheppy, the dog, giving chase to
the house cat, Lady Jane Grey, no less, and concludes with his
disgrace "after an argument with a skunk." An automobile ride
that reads like a parody of one of Dickens's descriptions of a
coach ride derides the "speed mania" of the modern world.
"Honk! Honk!...a woman hoeing in a field of sugar-beets
straightens her back to look at us for a moment and waves her
hand—or did she shake her fist at us?...Honk Honk....Past
fields of tomatoes planted under contract with the benign
Canners' combine."[18] These mock epics make their points lightly
and amiably. The form was good for McArthur, for it precluded his becoming unduly heavy-handed as in so much of
his late satire.

Nowhere else is this characteristic so obvious as in the satirical
aside, one of McArthur's favorite methods of attack. Lamentably
it frequently failed him. He tends to jeer, and his obsession with
politics and economics becomes tiresome. The humorous aside
normally added to the discussion. The suggestion of boiling a
calf to remove him from a fence is high-spirited nonsense, but
for all that, it is in context. The "flashes" of satire are often
obtrusive—wrong in tone and irrelevant as subject matter. In the
middle of a description of making a fire, one finds this comment:
"In a few minutes I had a bonfire that would have been big
enough to celebrate a victory over the Big Interests," or, in an
essay on chickens, that they are "like a mob of intelligent human
beings," they may "trample one another to death," and that, in
another, a rooster "acted for all the world like the leader of an
opposition that had suffered a humiliating defeat."[19]

McArthur had, to quote R. P. Baker on Haliburton, the
"shrewd, caustic qualities of the Scotch," and he displayed them
throughout his career in different degrees in his satire, which
changed from the refined and ironic to the often blunt and
sarcastic, as he grew older. The more entangled he was in the

affairs of the farm world, the more he allowed the purpose of satire to override the delight that theoretically it was to produce. The more satirical he became the less humorous he became. Conron's remark that McArthur's satire was frequently an unpleasant form of attack puts the case well as regards the later essays.[20] It tells only a half-truth, however, for in those early years in New York and London, McArthur, the satirist, produced works that belong with his very best.

IV *Laughter in Their Midst*

By 1911 McArthur had, he told Vaux, "won considerable reputation as a cheerful humorist," but he never succumbed to the temptation to become a professional "funny man," as he feared Leacock was in danger of becoming. He seldom wrote humorous essays for the sake of the humor, as in "Uniparous," and relatively few of the kind on any score. Vital and warmhearted as many of the essays are, McArthur used humor as seasoning rather than as a main dish, and he protested against those who missed his earnestness of intent and who, seeing only his humor, failed to read him correctly. Moreover, it was part of his philosophy that people should not depend on others for their amusement. (The pioneers had not done so.) He wanted each person to realize self, a function of idealism and a central concern of the simple life. Yet the paradox remained that he needed humor to help him make that way of living appear attractive. He required it to verify the truth of the "fun" that he maintained could be found in everyday work and events.

McArthur made little use of his old-time breadwinners, the epigram and the joke, in his farm essays, for he realized that neither fitted their style and outlook. Occasionally he sums up his argument with a short precise statement—"There is no danger of a confusion of tongues, because money talks in all languages"—or he tries to catch the atmosphere of a scene in a similar fashion—"I can see that nothing makes cramped quarters so overcrowded as a little touch of temper."[21] This technique, however, is the exception, not the rule. As regards jokes, McArthur uses one only when he wants a lighthearted illustration of a point or, as a simile, to give it another dimension. He never

regards it simply as a means of "warming the reader to him."
Once he did introduce an essay with a joke. It concerned an
American lady who was heartbroken because she "had to give
up the family mansion. It had been in the family for twelve
years."[22] The laugh was secondary since the story of the lady
became the theme of a discussion of the attitude of Canadians
toward their farms vis-à-vis English landed pride.

Canada has no distinctive farm jokes on which McArthur
could draw, nor probably would have wished to draw, for with
few exceptions he created his own humor. A few country jokes
show up—the farmers who work all summer to get enough money
to go to law with their neighbors in winter; the early trapper
who, seeing a wagon passing by in the far distance, moved
away because "the place was getting too crowded." Of course,
there are the jokes about the lady with the new bath who could
"hardly wait till Saturday night," and of the "tall-tale" farmer
who knew spring had arrived because the snow was "down to
the tops of the windows." The examples are few, for McArthur,
when he wanted to draw on others, much preferred to illustrate
his points with quotations from the poets rather than from the
humorists of the past.

Since McArthur wrote personal essays almost exclusively, his
humor runs the risk of becoming a self-centered life-with-father-
on-the-farm or boobs-in-the-woods sort of travesty. Fortunately,
he normally avoids this irritating sort of humor (which so often
characterizes "country stuff"); he loved and respected the
country and hoped to gain its love and respect, believing that
those who understood the true purpose of his work appreciated
him as a sincere spokesman for their cause. Behind the comic
mask was a serious-minded and sensitive man. His jocularity
was frequently, he told a correspondent, an act of will rather
than the spontaneous overflow of high spirits, a circumstance
that helped give his humor tension and depth. Moralizing about
a man who left his home town because people laughed at the
way he lit a cigar, McArthur comments epigrammatically:
"The business of amusing one's fellow men, when it is attended
by a little success is sometimes decidedly tragic."[23]

McArthur never gave up this "business." His humor indirectly
helped spread his philosophy of the simple life and gave him the

opening to say things that would otherwise have remained unsaid because of personal predilection or editorial edict. "Neither the Globe nor the Advocate," he told Vaux in a letter (October 16, 1914), "would publish my article. So I switched my attack to humor." Even when he centers his humor on himself it is rarely cute or merely clever. His secret lies in the fact that as a naïve commentator he pretends not to notice his flaws or considers them strengths. In addition, if he recognizes his flaws he seldom laughs at himself, thus conversely allowing the readers to enjoy his mishaps and failures.

At one time he is the easygoing rustic who always churns on Saturdays, unless the children happen to be home from school some other day; at another time he is the dilatory farmer, who, hiding his methods under mock elegance, speaks of a dead hen left in the snow as having been in cold storage for two months. Once he ran so far counter to farm tradition as to tell the farmers "How to Loaf," though the irony may not have been accidental. He chops off the limb on which he is standing, but admits his foolishness and consoles himself that silly actions help to keep people humble, and so by his very seriousness, not by self-indulgent laughter, he provokes laughter.

A tyro in the woods, he recognizes his inadequacies, but he avoids the obviously contrived in his descriptions of them. He is no show-off playing for laughs. His ability to root his humor in the actual precludes his misadventures from becoming slapstick buffooneries and his becoming a clown. Moreover, his humor is usually much more humor of character than of action. The essay on woodcutting begins with an enthusiast who needs exercise and believes that "a session at the end of a crosscut" is just the thing for him. Four pages later, the flagging enthusiast, who has at least proved himself an artful dodger, goes home, a sadder and a wiser man.

When the cut was finished I just had enough breath left to start a discussion of the comet that is now appearing in the west. The papers have not told definitely whether it is Halley's comet or another visitor. But even that ended.

After the next cut I managed to work up a talk about the plans of the Hydro-electric and to paint in glowing colours the good times we would have when electricity would be used to heat houses and for cooking. It wouldn't be necessary to cut wood then. Whew!

While the next cut was coming off a blister broke and I couldn't think of anything to talk about, so we plunged recklessly into another. Then I began to count the strokes. I found it took five hundred to take off one block. That may not show well beside some of the records made at the sawing matches, but it must stand. About this time I thought it would be a good idea to take the measuring stick and mark off the rest of the stub. Twenty-nine more cuts. At five hundred strokes to the cut, you can figure out what that would amount to. When I realized what this meant I sat on the log and, as Meredith says, my "thoughts began to bloat like poisoned toads." Would the sun never go down? I was killing time as shamelessly as a plumber. To work again, and then another blister broke. I don't believe the stories they tell about two men cutting eight cords of wood in a day with a crosscut saw.

As the dragging minutes passed I began to sympathize with Sisyphus, who had to roll a stone uphill, only to find it always rolled back. No matter how savagely I yanked that saw towards me, it would be yanked away. As I kept up the dreary task I began to admire Schopenhauer, and decided that henceforth I would be an outspoken pessimist. Still the saw whimpered—

"Tang, Tan-n-n-n-g!"

At last, when "even despair grew mild," I was told the time had come to do chores. Without a word I shambled towards home and, like Hosea Biglow, I went "Back / Along the very feetmarks of my shining morning track."[24]

Whatever the farmer appreciated of the use of both mock epic and burlesque in the conclusion and of the fine touch, "you can figure out what that would amount to," he would readily enjoy the portrait of the greenhorn.

V *Animal Comedy at Ekfrid*

The comedy played out at the Ekfrid farm fortunately gave McArthur chances to laugh, too, without the slightest need to laugh at himself, for his animals were good copy. Sometimes he was the target of a joke, but one played on him by Dolly, his driving horse, or Fenceviewer I, or that ever-famished pig, Beatrice. McArthur juxtaposes man with animals to deflate man, their "innocence" outdoing his "experience," but sometimes, with such eccentric beasts as his, he reveals the humor in a

situation in which he outwits one of them. Fenceviewer I, or II
(it matters little since II is a chip off the old block), swallows
a rubber ball in her gluttony, but after all McArthur's fretting
and abortive efforts to dislodge it, "she hastily picked up a nice
clean corn-cob and put it down as dessert to the rubber ball."[25]
Poor Dolly, the slow driver, fares much worse. She runs away
and leads her master a merry dance over hill and dale, but lacking the cunning of Fenceviewer falls prey to deceit herself when
McArthur tempts her with an ear of corn, but, having caught
her, plays a practical joke on her to even accounts, and refuses
her the tidbit, on the ground that she "might take it as a reward
for her exploit," thus incongruously defending his revenge as a
highly moral act.[26]

Humor of character as seen in the animal sketch, especially
as it relates to cows, is one of McArthur's strong points. In a
commentary aimed at Roberts and Seton, whose animals think
profoundly, he presents this psychoanalysis of bovine behavior.

Cows are deep. They think thoughts that are beyond the poets. You
can't fool me about cows, because I am living with them just now.
Acting as valet to a bunch of cows and young cattle has given me
a chance to study them closely, and my respect for them is increasing every day. Cows certainly think, but only when they have the
proper environment. They don't think all over the place like college
professors and eminent people generally. It has always been very
disconcerting to me to meet great men on the street, or in the railway station, or on the crowded rear platform of a street car, and
to find them thinking all the time. They seem to have developed
thinking into a bad habit, but not so with cows. Cows spend days
and days without thinking, but when conditions are right they think
unutterable things. And they are very human in this. A well-known
writer told me once that he can never think freely unless he begins
by thinking about a telegraph pole. He couldn't explain why it was,
but if he once got his mind completely concentrated on a telegraph
pole ideas would at once come surging into his brain. It is the same
with cows, and the object that inspires them to their loftiest flights
is a gate. Let no one be surprised at this. Even philosophers have
mighty things to say about gates. What says Omar?
  "Up from earth's centre to the Seventh gate
   I rose, and on the throne of Saturn sate,

And many a knot unriddled by the way
But not the master-knot of human fate."
Fate—there you have it. Fate is undoubtedly the favourite subject
of thought with meditative cows. You have only to look at them and
notice their awful solemnity and the gravity of their mild and magnificent eyes to know that they are not thinking of any ordinary
matter like the beef trust, or the high cost of hay, or anything of
that sort. But it is not enough to have a cow see a gate to start her
thinking. You must try to drive her through it.[27]

This passage epitomizes almost all the characteristics of Mc-
Arthur's humor of description, of "character," with a touch of
social satire as an aside, and of situation, with a quotation thrown
in as a masterstroke of incongruity. It is all good-natured nonsense, but the irony and irreverent tone give it a bite, poking
fun, as it does, at cows and mankind, at solemnity parading as
profundity, and at pseudo-intellectualism and pomposity.

In other essays McArthur stresses one or another of the various
kinds of humor exemplified in his tribute to cows. His animals
lent themselves readily to humor of character, since they were
largely type or flat characters with a "ruling passion" for food,
and to humor of situation, which dramatized their characteristics. They were almost always up to something; pigs stole oats
from the granary, cattle broke into and out of fields, and hens
scratched in the dooryard garden despite the threat of a bran-
dished broom—all in a plot that revolved around a domesticated
version of man's struggle with nature, or, often at Ekfrid, nature's
struggles with man. Occasionally McArthur's humor of situation
descends to farce, as in his account of bringing home a load of
honey pails and crates, or in his comments on golf, in which he
attempts to make fun of urban life with an exaggerated account
of the problems inherent in the game. Normally he avoids the
merely ludicrous and the run-of-the-mill humor of situation.
He was working in a new area.

At times his humor of description, when it is a set piece,
results in this kind of thing (he is writing of a stone the Indians
once used to crush grain): "If a marauding Iroquois surprised
the lady of the wigwam by poking his head through the opening
and looking at her with an engaging smile, she would doubtless
grab the family grist-mill and bounce it off his scalp-lock, in

the meantime accompanying the passionate gesture with an appropriate ceremonial war-whoop."[28] Here McArthur presents not only a smart-aleck self-conscious kind of verbal humor, but one that assumes the crude and cruel as comical, as Dickens sometimes assumes it. It appears in McArthur's accounts of his misadventures with his farm animals, one of which, describing his kicking and beating a pig, got him into hot water with several of the readers of the *Globe*, and runs back to "The Black Sheep Club," a short story of which McArthur thought highly and in which the "humour" depends on men being kicked downstairs.[29] Luckily such aberrations cannot nullify the general impression of geniality as McArthur's hallmark. As with humor of character in the essays about farm life, it never becomes humor of the grotesque (the so-called humor of caricature). His realism saved him from that. Besides, who could "caricature" animals, or would need to "caricature" McArthur's? They provided humor enough as they were.

The Red Cow is McArthur's only book that can be called a collection of humorous essays, as distinct from satire, and many of these were lighthearted rather than humorous, although often the mere presence of one of his animals is good for a smile.

VI *Seated with Haliburton and Leacock*

Normally McArthur lets his humor flicker here and there across his page. Sometimes he plays with words. He draws up lists to effect humor through exaggeration and any other device he can use with the list. "I am suffering," he writes, "from springhalt, spavins, saddle-galls, splints, and sore shoulders."[30] He coins words for purely verbal humor: "Like jelly that wouldn't jell or politics that wouldn't poll, my batch of butter wouldn't but."[31] Oddly enough, in view of the years he spent writing jokes, he excludes the pun almost entirely from his bag of humorous verbal tricks in his essays. Moreover, though his short stories reveal that he was a master of dialect, he rarely, if ever, resorts to it in his nonfiction.

By and large McArthur's humor depends little on the play of words in themselves. He uses few "funny" conceits and tries for effect not through "clever" phraseology but through comments whose humor depends on idea or the quick summation of character. At its worst it produces this sort of thing—a miniature tall tale: "The puddles may be half an inch deep or . . . so deep that chinamen are fishing in them from willow pattern bridges on the other side of the earth."[32] At its best it fuses understatement, exaggeration, and the incongruous to elicit that shock of surprise without which there is no wit. In the midst of a description, a reminiscence, a narrative, the reader comes across strange information. A steer, Mungo, for instance, "eats standing up at times . . . because when he is forced to get up he is too lazy to lie down";[33] and an optimistic young turkey, marooned "wishbone deep" in snow on the top of a haystack, "stood waiting for a thaw to come and rescue him."[34] Farmer McArthur had his problems, too, but humorist McArthur had the magic touch to turn them to good account. Plum jelly that is too sour to eat presents him no difficulty. He can use it to kill weeds on the lawn, or to feed to the pigs, if they are "so warped by the dry weather that you want to shrink them up so that they will hold swill."[35] With the same straight face he is frightened in an accident lest his "new cowhide shoes should be ruined by being driven through the cement floor" of the stable.[36] None of these exemplify wit in the sense that their humor depends on verbal effect, but all do exemplify their author's ability to yoke the incongruous together to produce a glow of humor in addition to the sparkle of wit.

As humorist, McArthur belongs with Haliburton and Leacock as the best in Canadian literature. He wrote much less humor than either, but the quantity is not negligible and the quality of his best work equals theirs. He entered the literary world when humor, if not king, was crown prince, when Nye, Billings, Ward, and Twain were entertaining thousands with their rough and tumble humor of tall tales, burlesques, and parodies, and for some time, like them, he tried to earn a living by making people laugh. His career as professional humorist lasted only a few years, however, for he dropped it to become an adherent and advocate of the simple life. He retained his sense of humor, though, and used it in his writing as a method of coating his didacticism or, more often, as a kind of comic relief to his "message."

Both Haliburton and McArthur were satirists, but McArthur is much less satirical in general than Haliburton. When satirical, he is normally blunter than the Nova Scotian, since Haliburton could call on Slick to help him carry the burden in the Clockmaker series, and the Old Judge was a tenderhearted fellow. McArthur never found himself bound to a character as Haliburton became to Slick and, hence, left himself the opportunity for a broader range of humor.

As compared with Leacock, McArthur was much quieter. Whereas Leacock joined the laugh parade with his boisterous and often flashy humor, McArthur preferred a friendly chuckle and the sly remark or the canny observation. If Leacock is correct that the Scottish tradition in humor centers in character, then McArthur demonstrates the truth of the comment. It is not only the focal point of much of his humorous writing, but the background also, for behind it all there is always visible an intelligent, witty, and kindly man.

CHAPTER 7

Farmer

I *"Country Stuff"*

M cARTHUR lumped his essays about rural life under one heading, "country stuff," but they differ much, falling into three generally distinct categories. Sometimes they center on the details of nature (both wild and domesticated); sometimes, on nature in the large; sometimes, on farm life. McArthur occasionally combines two or three of these categories in one essay and nearly all his essays at least touch on nature. Of all the books of "country stuff," *The Red Cow* alone is restricted almost entirely to the details of nature and to the animal life on the farmyard. The rest are mixed bags, *In Pastures Green* the best balanced of all with its discussions of the philosophy of nature, its accounts of Ekfrid flora and fauna, and its descriptions of the various pursuits and aims of farmer McArthur himself.

II *Field Naturalist*

McArthur wrote much about cows, horses, pigs, field crops, and even the lowly vegetable, but the creatures of the woods and fields with their trees and flowers also attracted him. All these gave him a feeling that neither farm activities nor any amount of stargazing or of Rousseauistic (or, perhaps better, Carmanian) reverie could induce. "The birds," he recorded joyfully, "are beginning to realize that my intentions are not hostile and show signs of accepting me into a fellowship of nature."[1] With this imaginative sympathy went also an inquisitive mind, and McArthur developed into a field naturalist of some ability for his day and age and certainly for a farmer. He had no Peterson Guide, no field glasses, and, unlike Thoreau, one of his favorite authors, kept no notebooks. The affairs of the natural

122

world were simply part of the life he had chosen to write about. He felt no need to peep and botanize unduly to enjoy them, and his work has the unsophisticated enthusiasm and breadth of interest typical of nature writing at its best.

"Our scientific men," he complained, "are all so serious-minded that I am afraid they miss many things when engaged in their nature studies. Perhaps if they cultivated humour a little they would not make so many solemn blunders."[2] McArthur held more than solemnity and mistakes against biologists and botanists. They made nature study into work and negated its pleasures. They tended, also, to remove something of the wonder of nature in their studies. They never saw heaven in a grain of sand. They disproved that horsehairs become eels, that thunder kills tadpoles, and that snakes charm birds, and thus exploded the cherished beliefs of childhood. McArthur protested less against accuracy of observation than against what he thought their limited involvement in making and recording it. He wished to transform nature study into an affair of the heart, head, and hand, to humanize science and to make farmers aware of the attractiveness of their environment, and in this way to help alleviate their stultifying labors. Science bothered him not because it brought the intellect to bear on nature—nature was not antithetical to the mind—but because it did not bring the feelings also.

The armchair naturalists, like the natural scientists, disturbed McArthur, for, if only a casual observer in general, he was often a keen observer of the specific. He respected fact for what it disclosed about the whole scheme of nature. He was not "afraid to bet," he said, "that a lot of the nature studies [appearing] in the papers have [little] foundation in fact."[3] Roberts and Seton were sometimes for him, as for Theodore Roosevelt, nature fakirs. They described animals capable "of matching the intelligence of man." They knew the inner thoughts of wolves and bears. Their "short-sighted heroes" also made McArthur dubious, for they could not "walk through a page of printed text without seeing game and making observations that would take [McArthur] hours of hunting and watching."[4]

At the other extreme from these people—the natural scientists who impassively observed the facts of nature and the armchair naturalists who invented them—stood the farmers, who "living more closely in touch with nature than any one else . . . probably enjoy her . . . less than any one else. Even the city man who goes for an occasional stroll in the park," McArthur conceded, "enjoys nature more than they do."[5] Here McArthur made a major concession, since the city signified so much he disliked, but his comment derives from his propaganda on behalf of ruralism, for he wished the farmers to establish a relationship with the natural world not only through field crops and livestock but through its sights and sounds, forms and colors. "Even a newly-turned clod," he declares, "its worthy of study for what it will reveal." No man, he asserts, really owns his farm "who does not know all its pleasant places . . . the shadiest tree . . . [the spots] where the hepaticas bloom and . . . green aisles of the woods are heavy with incense of phlox. He should," McArthur continues, "be acquainted with the robins that return to the same nest year after year," and, echoing Emerson's *Nature*, as if to give a balance to his praise of the clod, he extols the panorama of the countryside, which the eye, "open to beauty, and the enjoying mind can take as [their] own wherever [they] find] it."[6]

Despite this nonscientific attitude, McArthur, having grown up in the country, brought considerable knowledge to bear on his subject. To this nature lore, picked up incidentally, McArthur added bits and pieces from his reading. He knew C. W. Nash's work on the birds and E. J. Zavitz's, on the trees of Ontario, and other government bulletins pertaining to the rural world. He knew the work of Fabre, and John Burroughs, and of Hamilton Laing and Sam Woods, both of whom wrote nature study columns for the *Globe* when he was associated with it. He makes no mention of Audubon, but Thoreau he quoted often. Finally he had a chance in neighboring Glencoe to study specimens in one of those cases of "stuffed birds" once so much a part of the furnishings of the front parlors in nineteenth-century Southern Ontario homes.

Like most field naturalists McArthur made birds his specialty, and even kept a pet crow. They were ubiquitous and relatively easy to observe, almost a necessity for McArthur, if the following comment can be trusted (or even imagined by a birdwatcher). "A pileated woodpecker began calling in the west corner. I wanted to see him, but felt too restful to get up and hunt for him."[7] If lackadaisical at times about birding, McArthur could identify at least fifty-three species. Moreover, he liked to watch birds, not merely to list them. If no "lister," he did, nevertheless, appreciate the thrill of adding a new species to his life list. It meant more than another name to be totted up or a collection of field marks to be memorized, as his account of his first bald eagle indicates.

When I was within about forty yards of the tree my visitor stretched his neck and turned to look at me. It was a magnificent bald eagle— the first I had ever seen outside of a zoological garden. I was near enough to catch the glint of his fierce eye. He gave me "the once-over" with an expression of haughty disdain. . . . Then he turned toward the rising sun, leaned forward as if making obeisance, and launched himself into the morning with a wide beat of wings. He paid no attention to the pursuing crows. After a few powerful strokes he swung up on a vast spiral and sailed away to the east. Although he was so unsociable, I was glad to have seen him, and I had a really exciting story to tell the children when they got home from school in the evening.[8]

This is not a bird-guide portrait; for all its want of precision, however, it, like a Bruno Liljefors painting, as compared with one by Allan Brooks, or even Audubon or Louis Feurtes, catches the living bird with amazing realism. "Fierce eye," "leaned forward," "launch himself," and "wide beat of wings" are precise observations and remarkably accurate descriptive phrases. The spiral flight puts the bird in a new context of the totality of nature and adds to the impressiveness of the scene. As regards the tale for the children, it makes a neat escape for a grown man who wished to conceal that he was as excited as a child, and who, in trying to avoid showing his feelings, made more obvious how truly excited he was.

McArthur was much more interested in bird and animal behavior than in any other aspect of biology, and in this way his commentary on the eagle is typical. His books, however, include, not only many observations of the kind, but considerable bird lore that relates to the abundance and distribution of several different species. He writes consistently of the status of the quail and some other species in both pioneer and modern times. He notes the spread of the brown thrasher, the mocking bird, and Bartram's sandpiper (upland plover) into Southwestern Ontario at the turn of the century. Indeed, a collection of his commentaries on birds would make a worthwhile addition to the history of Ontario ornithology.

In other areas of field studies McArthur lacked the enthusiasm he had for birds, and, since wild animals are more difficult to observe and plants are not especially lively subjects, he wrote much less about either. Yet he kept fairly close tabs on the wild animals of his farm—particularly black squirrels and rabbits—and recorded no fewer than fifteen different species, including that most furtive creature, the flying squirrel. He could, moreover, identify several of these animals—red squirrel, black squirrel, weasel, mink, skunk, red fox, raccoon, and mice (probably field mice)—by their tracks, a feat of some difficulty that reveals his ability in the field and something of the pioneer state of the world in which McArthur lived.

Now and then he turned to such unpretentious kindred of the wild as toads, snakes, turtles, and crayfish; although they did not figure extensively in his nature diary, some of these lowly creatures provided him with material for excellent literary-scientific essays in the manner of Gilbert White. "Snake and Frog," for example, reveals the same keen observation, the same inquisitive mind, and the same direct prose that marked the work of the old English naturalist, as this section, which is representative of the whole, demonstrates:

I understand that the old belief that snakes charm or hypnotize their prey has been exploded; but why on earth did that frog stand there within striking distance of the snake when the other frogs were hopping to safety? Was it so paralyzed by fear that it could not move? And the snake evidently had its attention so concentrated on the frog that it did not realize the danger of exposing itself so recklessly while I was within striking distance. It evidently looked on that frog as its dinner, and was so intent on its plans that it overlooked the rule of Safety First. I was unable to stay and watch for further developments, but I am wondering if our common garter snakes ever plunge into the water in pursuit of frogs. Under ordinary circumstances the frogs would have dived to safety, but the approach of the snake caused them all to jump out of the pool. This makes it seem as if they were afraid of capture if they remained in the water. I have seen garter snakes swimming across a stream, though I never suspected that they might be in the water for the purpose of hunting game. While I did not acquire any new knowledge while indulging in this nature study, I discovered how little I know about snakes and frogs when it comes to matters of life and death.[9]

As a farmer McArthur concerned himself of necessity with insects. Indeed, he looked on farming as "a bug fight," and his concern with entomology was largely a discussion of species injurious to crops. In writing of them he was more objective and factual than in most of his other observations of nature. They scarcely lent themselves to his romantic idealism, but, through study of them, he came to appreciate the achievement of the biological sciences and their practical value to the farmer. He learned, for example, the life of the codling moth and marveled at the way in which science used its knowledge to control this scourge of the orchards through the simple expedient of spraying. "Borgias, de Medicis, and Brinvilliers," he notes, "were clumsy poisoners compared with scientists who protect the bounties of nature from the ravages of prodigal hordes. Poisoning the blossom for the unborn insect is surely the masterpiece of protective science."[10] After World War I he convinced himself and tried to convince others that a world famine was in the offing; that the war between man and insect was of even greater consequence than the bloody years 1914–1918 had been, and, in one long alarmist essay, "The New War," even warned that "the existence of the race is threatened."[11] The greatest enemies were the corn borer, the Hessian fly, and potato beetle, and he made them the subjects of factual and practical comments.

More typical of McArthur were his essays on crickets and grasshoppers, and even *Perillus bioculatus*. In them he was more imaginative and subjective. He liked to watch the turkeys as they stalked grasshoppers in the fields and enjoyed listening to the crickets round about the dooryard. As for *Perillus bioculatus*, an introduced potato beetle parasite, he cheerfully renamed it the "Fun Bug," since it would reduce the work of the farm.

Here he demonstrates once again his respect for biological and botanical sciences and, again, without ever noting that the benefits of their work derived indirectly from peeping and botanizing. Nor did he foresee what, in *Silent Spring*, Rachel Carson was to record of the devastation wrought by poison as a means of fighting a "bug war." Pleased with the way in which spraying had destroyed the codling moth in his orchard, he was sure that the scientists' proper work was "devising means for overcoming disease and fighting pests."[12]

McArthur knew the trees of his area. He could identify at least thirty-one species, among which was the now extremely rare Canadian sweet chestnut, and many, even red and white oaks, by their shapes. As with the birds and animals, he was often highly subjective when writing of the trees—once again more humanist than scientist, for his studies of trees never concerned bark texture, leaf counts, bud sizes, shapes, and colors. His feelings ran deep, and his moving essay "My Friends, the Trees" provides a key to the associational basis of much of his nature study, as this passage from the essay suggests:

Near the house there is a sturdy oak tree that I always think of as one of the oldest of my friends. I grew up with it. Of course, that is not exactly true, for I stopped growing many years ago while it kept on growing, and it may keep on growing for centuries to come. But when I was a growing boy it was just the right kind of a tree for me to chum with. It was not too big to climb, and yet it was big enough to take me on its back and carry me to all the dreamlands of childhood. Among its whispering branches I found lands as wonderful as Jack climbed to on his beanstalk. And it had a stout right arm that was strong enough to hold a swing on which I swung and dreamed for more hours than the teachers of to-day would consider right. When it whispered to me I whispered to it, and told it more secrets than I have ever told any one in the world. It became a part of my life, and no matter how far I wandered in later years my thoughts would always return to the tree in times of sickness and trouble. I always felt that I would be well and happy again if I could only get back to the tree and throw myself at full length on the grass that it shaded and listen to its neverending gossip with the breezes that are forever visiting it. At last I came back from the outer world and made my home beside the tree. During my absence it had pushed up higher and had spread its branches wider, but it was still the same companionable tree. The grass still made a carpet over its roots, inviting me to sprawl at full length and renew our voiceless communion. While I was away I may have learned some things, but the tree had been in harmony with the universe from the moment it began to emerge from the acorn, and knew all that I so sorely needed to learn.[13]

Nothing on the farm escaped McArthur's notice. He knew the meadows and the woodland nooks where phlox, violets, Indian turnips, hepaticas, adder's tongues, trilliums, Dutchman's breeches, and mayflowers grew. Under the guidance of his son, "a boy engaged in nature study," he learned to identify Solomon's seal, miter-wort, foam-flower, and many others, whose "college names" he was sure he would not remember when he met the flowers again. Yellow violets, dogtooth violets, spring beauties, bloodroot, pepper root, and May apples were also names on his list, which in toto makes a fine record of the wild flowers that thronged the farm woodlots of old Ontario years ago. As might be expected, wild raspberries, thimbleberries, and strawberries, which McArthur says he loved to pick, were superior to the garden varieties.

McArthur knew many farm weeds, but groused little about them and even categorized and discussed the goldenrod as a beautiful wild flower. The tenacity of weeds, and especially of grass, impressed him more than their identities. Bindweed, he averred, could be killed only by building "a barn with a cellar about eight feet deep on the spot . . . with a solid cement floor."[14] On a more serious level he feared grass as a demonstration of a blind force in nature. "The grass has grown over those who are dear to us, and it will grow over us. And this is the same grass that makes the summer laugh with beauty."[15] This was a passing mood, but it reveals some of the background from which McArthur's essays on nature derive. They were no shallow celebrations of the merely pretty.

The horticulturists McArthur thought unobservant. All their new grains required pampering, which was not nature's way, and he cited the weeds to prove his point and to suggest that scientists plant their new strains of seeds among the weeds and allow natural selection to produce the best. "Think of what a boon it would be," he dreams, "to have grains that would grow like weeds without cultivation of any kind and still yield good crops."[16] McArthur never ceased to marvel, either, at the process of photosynthesis, and described it fully as a machine run by sunlight. The miracle of plant fertilization, which the horticulturists could almost pattern, provided him also with the opportunity to "teach" the farmers some botany and to try to instill in them some appreciation at least of the wonders of nature open to rational explanations.

III   The Red Cow and Other Recalcitrants

The world of bird and beast that McArthur knew best and that entertained him most was of course his own barnyard. To the observation that he was beginning to be accepted into the fellowship of nature he should have added that he had already accepted the farm animals into the fellowship of man. He believed that they had personalities of their own. Others had observed this, but none, until McArthur, had been able to make literature of them and farm life. When commenting on a poor blackbird that had eaten kernels of corn that had been tarred and covered with ashes he described his way of analyzing animal behavior and character. "I merely try to imagine what I would do and say if some one whom I had helped . . . put coal tar in my salad. . . . Making my observations in this way I have no compunctions about explaining the state of mind of the blackbird. . . ."[17]

The issue McArthur is debating here has far less interest now than in the days when the animal story was popular, but the comment explains much of his success in presenting the Red Cow and the rest of his farm menagerie. Although he is writing of a blackbird in the passage quoted, his observation applies more readily to his approach to domesticated than to wild animals. He once had "an interview with a black squirrel," but got no copy from it, and he argued that a killdeer nesting in his pasture had a sense of humor and liked to tease Sheppy, the farm dog, but he generally never attempted to get inside the minds of wild creatures. It is quite otherwise with the farm animals, for he tried consistently to reveal their characters. On one or two occasions he even put their thoughts into words. He denied being a nature fakir, however, and drew a distinction between himself and Roberts and Seton. He objected to their undue anthropomorphism, as already mentioned, though he would not have dreamed, nor would have Roberts, surely, that Roberts's animals are most significant as human archetypes and that the death of the ox in his story "Strayed" symbolizes the fall of man, as some recent critics assert.

Here, of course, McArthur touched on a problem that his dealing with domesticated creatures helped to preclude. Roberts and Seton could not know and make friends with wild animals as he knew and made friends with his domesticated animals. They had to generalize. Since they were also trying to teach natural history, in which all animals are alike, and, if writing fiction, to demonstrate some theme about the wild, they were again forced to depict type rather than individual characters. They tried to overcome the difficulty by creating a kind of romantic hero or villain—the extraordinary—and by presenting him in an unusual predicament usually associated with death. McArthur simply wrote about the ordinary in their daily lives. He presented the "personality" of a separate creature, not the biography of a species and not an illustration of some aspect of its behavioral pattern or of some facet of a philosophy of nature. The result is that McArthur's animals have a vitality and verisimilitude that those of other nature writers, including Grey Owl, never quite achieve.

McArthur's farm was old-fashioned and provided a large cast for a never-ending drama with cows, horses, pigs, goats, sheep, cats, dogs, and chickens—White Leghorns, Devonshire game, Andalusians, Brahmas, Anconas, Buff Orpingtons, White Wyandottes, and Plymouth Rocks—bantams, guinea hens, ducks, and turkeys (and none ever raised on wire) as *dramatis personae*. Many of the animals bore names (often given by McArthur's children), but none such as "Rosy," "Blossom," and "Cherry," once popular for cows before scientific agriculture replaced names with numbers. The barnyard fowl, except for a chicken that the children designated "Uniparous," remained nameless. McArthur was too much of a dirt farmer to fall prey to the cuteness of some modern nature writers. No geese of his would he have ever called "Windrack" and "Lodestar." Often the names he gave his animals, as to the cows "Fenceviewer I" and "Fence-viewer II" (taken from the title of the old-time municipal fence inspector), served to sum up character, to comment ironically on it, like the sobriquets once common in the country. (He called his goat "Sir Clifford Sifton," however, in order, as he said, to get Sir Clifford Sifton's goat.) The names of McArthur's animals, also, like the tags of Dickens's characters, established character identity quickly and made it stick in the reader's memory.

In some ways *The Red Cow* is a cabinet of characters. The horse, Dolly, a "driver" (now an obsolete term for an obsolete animal, since its job was to pull a buggy), figures largely as the farm "cutup"; Beatrice, a pig, as "Gluttony," the sixth of the Seven Deadlies; Fenceviewer I, the deceitful and cunning; and Bildad, a pup, the youthful and innocent. McArthur created some tension in his book, not through the opposition of good and evil, but through normal behavior as opposed to the venial and to high-spirited peccadilloes. To emphasize this kind of analysis, however, does the book an injustice. His animals are always animals, individuals first and types second only. There has been many a breachy cow, but another Fenceviewer I? (None; unless Fenceviewer II.) Many voracious pigs, but ever another "Beatrice" who "recognizes" only the law of supply and demand? Ever another Bildad? Dolly? McArthur succeeds here because of his realism. He knew how to select details so as to create a living creature and to differentiate it from another, even of the same breed (as witness his two pigs, "Beatrice" and "The Speedhound"), and to relate anecdote and adventure stories with remarkable appropriateness to the animal concerned.

Here the old gobbler "stands" for his portrait: "In spite of his complaints the gobbler is still looking after his duties as a father. A little while ago when the sun was hot I saw him standing beside his flock tail down, head pulled in like a turtle's, and his wings spread out. He had converted himself into a sort of feathered pergola, under which his children might have taken shelter. But they paid no attention to him. Under the busy and clucking guidance of the old hen they were pursuing the elusive fly and other appetizing insects."[18]

IV *Man and Nature*

McArthur was never content merely to report facts. He set them in contexts that revealed them in a new light, and, in terms of natural history, often related them to matters pertaining to conservation. He belonged with no sentimentalist school. Some readers considered him unsympathetic toward birds and animals, and up to a point, they were justified, for McArthur was a man of his time in some of his attitudes toward wild creatures. He assumed, like many farmers, a hierarchy in nature that was determined by the economic value of any species. In this classification, vermin forms the lowest order. Among its members McArthur listed rats, mice, minks, skunks, woodchucks, rabbits, weasels—characterized by their "evil heads"—hawks, crows, sparrows, blackbirds, and blue jays. He refused to include robins, however, even if they were enemies of cherries that should be warded off with a gun, according to one contemporary horticulturist. McArthur preferred and advocated "shaking a broom at them with wrathful cries." For those species McArthur considered vermin, he did recommend and adopt the death penalty; weasels ate chickens; rabbits girdled apple trees. Sparrows wasted food. A dead sparrow was a good sparrow and worth the two cents a bird he paid his son to shoot them with his "Christmas rifle." He knew that hawks were vermin and, with no less authority than his admired Jack Miner thundering against their evil ways, he "oiled up his shotgun and laid in a store of ammunition" in the name of his barnyard fowl, and he even shot crows for scarecrows in the nesting season.

Sometimes he declared war on vermin, not on ecological but on humane grounds, for their predations on other species. He once shot a blackbird for molesting his dooryard robins. Sparrows drove native birds from their nests. Blue jays were nuisances. Cowbirds distressed him for their habit of laying their eggs in the nests of other birds, and, in a passage reminiscent of Alexander Wilson's and of Audubon's famous descriptions of flocks of passenger pigeons, he discusses these avian parasites:

One day when driving to the village I noticed a flock of these feathered parasites around a pasturing cow. As nearly as I could judge with my eye the flock was about four rods long and a rod wide. The

ground seemed black with them, but supposing that only one stood
on each square foot we can make calculation of the number in the
flock. Four rods equal sixty-six feet—one rod sixteen and a half feet—
say sixteen. Sixteen times sixty-six (I had to take a pencil to finish
the sum) gives one thousand and fifty birds or rather square feet
on each of which a bird stood. Let us say there were one thousand
birds. Each of these during the nesting period probably crowded
out from four to five young song sparrows or other small birds. So
that one flock of useless, pestiferous cow-birds probably meant the
death of three to four thousand useful song birds. No wonder our
scientists advise us to shoot cow-birds at sight.[19]

Despite evidence to the contrary, McArthur's bark was much
worse than his bite. He threatened for years to destroy the sparrows' nests in his barn, but never quite got around to it. He sided
with the cranes against the trout in that perennial sportsman's
argument. If he advocated the destruction of vermin, he never
did so on behalf of "saving" game species. His nature was not
definable in terms of creel and bag limits. A reformed hunter, he
tended to look askance at sportsmen. They destroyed the quail
and black squirrels. Moreover, he almost always identified them
as city people out to deprive the rural world of its rights. As
the years passed McArthur reconsidered his attitude toward
hawks, since they were "mostly the friends of man," and he
wondered, too, whether or not great horned owls, those night-
time raiders of hen and turkey roosts, ought not to be protected.
"As a nature lover" he pondered over his whole attitude toward
nature. "The bug," he admitted, "probably enjoys life just as
much as the turkey, and I wonder if the bug should not have
my sympathy rather than the birds." Such "a delicate point" he
was willing, however, "to leave to professors of ethics...."[20]
McArthur concerned himself with preservation as well as
conservation of wildlife. He worried that there seemed no place
left in the order of things for raccoons, nor for black squirrels,
once so common about Ekfrid that they were hunted with
switches, and he tried to keep the hunters from his farm. (He
wanted to restock his lands with quail, but did not know how.)
He protested against the picking of wild flowers lest they be
exterminated. Of greater concern was the preservation of farm
woodlots, and he almost pleaded with the farmers to enclose

them against grazing. He had known the forests of the pioneer era, when they were considered an enemy. Now there were only rags and tatters of their former magnificence, and he strongly argued for safeguarding the little that remained. A protected woodlot, he pointed out, provided a sanctuary for birds, "which are the natural and best bug controllers," a typical "nineteenth-century" comment about birds. He maintained, too, that a reforested area was an investment that all farmers should make in their lands, and set an example by replanting two acres of his fifty-acre farm.

McArthur did not argue directly for reforestation on the basis that a woodlot is beautiful. He seldom followed that line in any of his discussions of conservation. He knew that he had to emphasize the practical for his farm readers, but did not argue for reforestation in terms of water tables, flood control, or soil erosion. He tried to promote it directly as a "contribution to the service of future generations." Even here he knew he was on thin ice and held forth a hope that might convince the most materialistic that "some of the more rapid growing varieties . . . may be of use to me within the age-limit of the Psalmist." McArthur wished to keep the farming community free of the city coal merchant and the "strongly-asserted rights of Labour organizations and organized capital."[21] Independence, as much as conservation, then, formed the grounds for his reasoning. A woods properly managed could help keep a farm as self-supporting as in the days of the early settlers.

Whatever concept of conservation McArthur held, he based it largely on a recognition that the days of pioneer prodigality had gone. If, in some ways, he belonged to his age in his attitudes toward nature, as in arguing for conservation on economic grounds and damning some species as vermin, in other ways he surpassed the majority of farmers in his concern about the environment, and he opened the eyes of many to the important problems associated with man's guardianship of the natural world in the modern age.

On a different level, McArthur added another dimension to his essays about nature by placing it in the context of history and of the recollections of his youth. Sometimes, and strangely, since he was addressing himself to rural Canada, he placed his

nature study in a setting of classical antiquity, on one occasion
turning a commentary on the grasshoppers that swarmed his
fields into a brilliant discussion of Tithonus, and, on another,
making a beautiful sunny morning when "the air was full of the
happiness of birds" into a clever and original defense of
Diogenes. Sometimes he turned to early Canadian social history
and discussed the wild creatures in terms of their significance
to the settlers as diversion and often as profit and sustenance.
McArthur lamented that these same people had had no thought
of protecting wildlife "in those evil days, when to see a black
squirrel was to run for a gun."[22] He remembered those days and
grieved that the natural world he had known had all but passed
away, its forest reduced to woodlots, its stream to a government
drain, its grouse and deer gone, its squirrels scarce, and its
quail now but an errant covey or two. But they were all he had
left, and he almost always wrote nostalgically of them. Like
his woodlot, as symbols of the past, they put him in touch with
a world he had known and wished to revitalize.

Another frequent point of reference in McArthur's nature
writing was the contemporary world of politics and economics,
and he usually made nature a comment on it in the same satirical
spirit that he had used in his "Farm Fables." The fables, being
fiction, differed, of course, in their mode of social criticism from
that sprinkled through his nature essays, for in these it was little
more than a caustic remark that seldom reached the level of
humor. McArthur could spot a Big Interest behind almost every
bush. Crows cawing reminded him of politicians. Aphids on
the apple trees resembled bankers in the farming community.
Mosquitoes, especially "railway" mosquitoes, had the qualities
needed by good lobbyists. The examples are almost endless.
Only once did this kind of analogical reasoning produce a full-
length essay, "Nature's University." Whimsical without being
coy and satirical without being blunt, the essay differs greatly
from most cases in which McArthur uses nature to comment
derisively on man. McArthur is least satisfactory in this kind of
nature writing. He cannot reconcile the satirical aside with his
feelings for nature, for the comparison with what he disliked
in the human world axiomatically puts the natural in a bad light.

Furthermore, the societal asides, even if clever, detract from the general effect of a nature essay.

V *The Grandeur of Nature*

Despite the comment about being accepted into the fellowship of nature, McArthur for the most part takes nature into the fellowship of man, through his work, field study, history, and memory, and through comments on politics and economics. Frequently, however, he tried to get in touch with the spirit he thought permeated the natural world. He did not want, he wrote, to lease a private wire to the invisible, but to know "the visible, and tangible, and audible, and smellable and tasteable world," for the senses formed the first rungs on the ladder leading to communion with something that bound the natural world together and gave it meaning:

As you learn to look outward from yourself and to dwell less in your mind, that is so apt to breed cares and foolish worries, you will presently find your environment moving farther back and your life expanding. Your mind will presently be reaching out for the things that are beyond the immediate touch of your senses, and you will begin to realize what a mysterious and wonderful world you are living in. Your interest will gradually reach out to the stars and the universe itself.[23]

Since McArthur had no "horrid" mountains and gloomy forests to awe him as he gazed over the farmlands of Ekfrid township, he found it relatively easy to find a response in nature in the large to his desire for peace and contentment or to his aspirations of infinity. Sometimes the woods seemed to take him into its secret heart of solitude and to give him "something of their peace and accord with nature," and always in autumn the whole countryside was an open window on the essence of beauty.

Sometimes "a sunny day would strengthen and purify" McArthur and give rise to "promptings . . . not accounted for" in his philosophy, evoking passages from the great poets and persuading him of the spirituality involved in sun worship. Once a pair of hawks that circled up and up from the woods till they passed from sight set him wondering, and he asked himself, "What aspiration guided them in their high flight? Was it the impulse of Titan life to escape from its prison house?"[24] Like Arnold, McArthur, too, knew the feeling of exaltation (and occasionally of personal insignificance) that scanning the starry skies can give rise to. Yet he never saw man as a lonely and alien spirit, his kinship with nature restricted to the life force. More than an animate thing among other animate things, man always sought to identify with something bigger than self, and on the highest level could find it in and through nature.

McArthur was too honest and meditative a man, too much a man of the nineteenth century—that period when biology was the most significant concern of both religion and science—to close his eyes and mind to the problems that an acceptance of man's kinship with nature presented. He knew what science was saying, but also what he saw, felt, and intuited about nature, and he tried to fashion a philosophy that would take into account, if not reconcile, what appeared as contradictions between the different views. He recognized the threat to any concept of the kinship of nature posed by "the conceit which makes man regard the world as anthropocentric . . . [and] think that his life is the only one that matters in a world where all things are alive. . . ."[25] Believing that man's happiness depends on cooperation with, not domination over, nature, he knew the danger to man in practical terms when he disturbs the balance of nature.

McArthur based much of his philosophy of nature on vitalism. He proclaimed that he knew and felt that "the world is flooded . . . with the 'elan vital' of Bergson. . . ."[26] A "growing and building force," it made everything that stirs with life a temple and acted as "the compelling inspiration of all art and poetry and beauty."[27] It pervaded all animate nature, but was something apart from the physicochemical changes that take place in growth. It was "something that compels these changes, but does not enter into the combination itself," something that the scientists have made no more of than have the poets.[28] The latter, nevertheless, have long recognized that it is "as real powerful and subtle as electricity," as "an impalpable flame that inspires instead of consuming."[29] Normally McArthur associated the life force with joy, but he was human enough to have honest doubts about his "faith." The life force, he admitted, took no sides, but then argued that it was freely at the service of man and worked against him when he got control of it "to create woe and desolation."[30]

He did not leave the problem of the morality of nature there. If, at times, he appreciated the therapeutic influence of the woods, he discerned, also, their "smiling taciturnity," the primitive in them, which, perhaps, did not deny the human entirely, as the forests of Maine had seemed to Thoreau to deny it, but which certainly did not "invite the fellowship of man." He did not want to draw on nature for morals as Seton did in *The Natural History of the Ten Commandments* and he even grumbled about Shakespeare's "sermons in stones," which, he thought, attributed to nature far too palpable a design on man. He wanted to believe that "all operated for the common good," but did not shy away from facts that seemed to deny such belief.

The contemplation of the cowbird's destructive parasitism drove the question home sharply, and he confesses his perplexity unabashedly. "Truly it is as hard," he laments, "to draw moral reflections from nature as from man. All seems bound up in the same cruel mystery. . . ." (He made this remark during World War I.) Then, as if to salvage something of his most cherished faith, he continues, "though we may some times have a vision of better things when we try to rise to the perfect enjoyment of a perfect day."[31] In ending thus, McArthur simply gives a secular version of the central admonition, "the leap into faith," of his early religious training, for his conclusion derives from his acceptance of nature as the revelation of a benevolent spirit despite apparent denials, much as the church bases its faith in a loving God regardless of seeming contradictions.

Darwin's theory presented a challenge to McArthur's belief in a moral nature, but throughout his career he tried to come to terms with it as a biological hypothesis. He accepted the concept of evolution and held that all "from the deep-hidden crystal in the rock to the screeching eagle participate in the scheme."[32] He admired the woodchuck, he ruefully conceded, because in its evolution, in contrast to man's, it had become a "fat rascal" "living in clover" and sleeping instead of worrying. Again, as McArthur studied the "impudence" of twelve little

pigs in their search for food and considered the success of the
meaner and more cunning in both the natural world and human
society, he felt convinced of the truth of evolutionary ethics.

Despite these concessions, McArthur could not accept "survival of the fittest" as the goal of evolution. He had described
it as "somewhat disappointing" in *The Sufficient Life*. He understood the food chain, "the incredible interdependence of nature,"
and noted that "wasteful, inefficient, illogical nature," when
viewed in the proper light, is "miraculously efficient."[33] He was
no nambypamby about nature; he accepted it as it is, but could
not accept survival as its only meaning:

In this country you can see the struggle for existence everywhere.
Everything from the tenderest herb to the beast of prey destroys
something else so that it may live; while nature seems to exist
solely for the reproduction of life she seems to value none. From the
highest to the lowest each living thing is in time destroyed as
unconcernedly as it was created. Natural life is an endless comedy
of reproduction; an eternal tragedy of change in death. And to what
end? The survival of the fittest? Nonsense! It is mere presumption
on the part of any man to pretend to know which is the fit and
which the unfit. . . . If you say that it means the survival of the
fittest for the struggle for existence you are still talking nonsense.
The Tower of Siloam is falling all the time in the realm of nature,
and it destroys what you would call the fit and the unfit alike. The
hoof of a cow may accidentally destroy the best-equipped bug in all
your fields. It has no more chance for survival than the weakest. The
only thing that seems enduring in nature is life, and neither the form
nor type in which it survives seems of importance. Looked at in the
light of science, nature is as hideous and terrible as a nightmare.[34]

Although the passage misinterprets "survival of the fittest"
and confuses its meaning with the simple fact of death, it
demonstrates McArthur's dissatisfaction with an approach to
nature that would put it in a scientific straitjacket. He wished
to believe evolution was teleological in some way, forever "leading upward and outward," its final goal a freedom in which
the material world becomes transformed into the spiritual. He
does not refer to God as the end of process, though he once
speaks of Him as the "Great Partner." If not sure of the ulti-

mate end, he believed, like his admired Tennyson, that things do seem "intelligible and part of one great plan that is working out for the good of all."[35] Finding little in the church to hang on to, or in science, since it posited a closed system and denied what he had emotionally and intuitively experienced as true, McArthur had to turn elsewhere for spiritual support, to nature, where he could keep in touch with the spirit of the world, and to history, where he found the human values that he cherished in the story of the pioneers. Moreover, in the simple life he discovered both fused to form a foundation for his faith.

VI *The Urban Challenge*

Frequently in the style of an early nineteenth-century romantic McArthur tried to bolster the cause of the simple life, not by praising the country, but by criticizing the city. Sometimes his attacks read like the old-time country school debates on the merits of the horse and the car. One spends more money living in the city and even at that does not have an opportunity to eat as well as the farmer. One cannot easily satisfy a wish to garden in a city, and, if one does, one acts as if playing with a toy (as McArthur points out in a sneery satire based on his sense of superiority over the office worker).

He presents a better image of himself and argument in this comment:

In the country a man may safely allow himself to be interested, but in the city it is different. The matter of interesting people has been reduced to a science. If one's attention is attracted by an attractive splotch of colour on a billboard he will soon find himself convinced that he should go to some lecture, concert, or movie show. Something interesting in a show window will cause him to pause, and before he realizes what has happened he will find that he is almost persuaded to buy something that he really does not need and perhaps cannot afford.[36]

Worse still the city was the seat of profit-gatherers, "efficient as pick-pockets," who as lords of the food markets and partners of the villain "Uncontrolled Capital" duped the farmer and the city laborer alike. McArthur knew these to be facts from his own experience, but could call Clarus Ager's *The Farmer and the Interests, a Study in Parasitism* (1916) to witness for doubting Thomases. It was the realm, too, of the bankers and the captains of industry, those men whose lives revolved around ideals that denied those of the simple life, and the demesne of the wealthy and sophisticated who, McArthur held, when his old-time puritan dander was up, revel and riot in luxurious ease.

If McArthur condemned the city for what it was in itself, he also criticized it for its intrusion into the rural world so as to lure the country folk, especially the young, from their homes and their way of life. Through contemporary art and literature it fostered foolish dreams of "military uniforms, places on boards of directors, and well-dressed triumphs of all kinds that are adequately applauded by beautiful women dressed in the latest fashion."[37] Newspapers played their part in rural decay, too, since they, McArthur asserted, generally neglected the country and, of course, attempted to make their cities appear attractive. As a youth, McArthur had obeyed the call of the city, only to find his dreams turn to ashes. He felt qualified, then, to warn others of the pitfalls of "Babylon," or rather the disappointments they would encounter there, for McArthur, though following an early romantic tradition, kept free of "poor Nellyism," focusing his interest largely on urban economic and cultural influences.

The glamour of the city he discounted as glitter unconnected in any way with happiness. In addition, young men going to the city could anticipate the pleasures of "a boiled horse boarding house" and the joy of debilitating physical labor in a factory or desiccating mental work in a business office, and since few were equipped for the latter, most were foredoomed to the menial and the routine. He had a warning, also, for any who wished to sell out and retire to the city, as was customary with older farmers years ago. He would find living expensive there, and greater comforts on the farm than he would "ever get on the back streets of any town or city."[38] Worst of all he would thenceforth lead an aimless existence.

Economic imperialism of the city posed a threat to agrarian life, but it could be put in simple terms. The farmer had become its tool and victim. The effect of those other urban influences,

science and technology, on rural society, however, lent itself
to no such facile summary. The natural sciences passed muster
when devoted to aiding the farmer, as with bulletins on the
development of new grains and livestock breeds, on weed and
pest control, improved methods of farming, and animal hus-
bandry. McArthur disliked the language of science, but appreciated the merit of these publications. He made little pretense
that he was trying to set himself up as a model scientific farmer,
but cast himself rather in the role of advocate. He knew the
farmers' language and "translated" these bulletins for them in
an attempt to persuade them to keep abreast of modern agron-
omy. For his efforts he got "on an average of three letters a day
from the farmers and even their wives and daughters" and once
received high commendation from the Deputy Minister of Agriculture of Ontario "for doing more to popularize scientific farming than anything else."[39] Nor did McArthur hesitate to castigate
those farmers who, "having worked hard and gained a little
success are convinced that book learning and science are
nonsense."[40]

Beyond this level of practicality, the natural sciences were on
thin ice. They tended to denigrate the simple life with their
talk of "vitamines—water-solubles A, B and C, and all the
rest...."[41] With their facts and theories they negated the
therapeutic and aesthetic values and, ultimately, the morality
of nature, turning life into a senseless whirligig of reproduction
and survival.

A similar ambivalence marked McArthur's assessment of the
achievements of technology. The telephone was both a friendly
thing and an ill-mannered and gossipy gadget that, like many
other inventions of the kind, got between people and living.
"Now," he declares, "about the only thing that is getting more
complex every day is the art of living. When we try to improve
it we add something—put in a telephone or something of the
kind—and keep on adding until we make life a burden."[42] Thanks
to horse-drawn implements and steam-driven machines city
manufacturers had much reduced the bull-work of farming, but
McArthur dampened his enthusiasm with a sprinkling of doubt.
The implement and the machine had alleviated farm labor, but
they had also, he feared, undermined the neighborliness of the

farming community. They also often reduced farming itself to a struggle with the "ravenous mortgage" that purchasing modern farm equipment seemed so frequently to require and they were destroying the basis of rural economy, since commercialism and industrialism were rapidly becoming the yardsticks of the value of the dollar.

If Mr. Massey and Mr. Ferguson, the two big manufacturers of farm implements, received only a lukewarm welcome from McArthur, they fared better than Henry Ford, whose infernal contraption McArthur damned as the epitome of all the worst of modernity, even proposing petrol control if it would free the highways of this menace. Speeding along the dusty country roads, the automobile symbolized for him the reality of urban intrusion into the rural world. It represented a shallow and privileged society whose only aim was to kill time, and, as a creation of science (a city affair like big business) it signified the threat of the scientific to the humanistic, the mechanical to the organic, the industrial to the agrarian. The years 1914–1918 only increased McArthur's uncertainty about the benefits of the machine and the future of mankind, for in that period he had seen the warlords, the captains of industry, and misdirected scientists united in a campaign of unbelievable carnage and devastation.

Living in an age that looked on science as a sacred cow, McArthur reveals some of the influences of the "faith," despite his reservations about technology and Darwinism. The struggle for survival explains the meaning of life in scientific or rational terms, he admitted, but he refuted it because he felt that "over all there brooded a spirit that was intensely aware—One without whose knowledge not even a sparrow could fall to the ground unnoticed."[43] Similarly the discoveries of science impressed him and left him dissatisfied.

The material progress of the world seems to depend strangely on their work [i.e., of scientists], even though they may have in mind nothing but the problems in hand. Great industrial enterprises have been made possible by this or that discovery in chemistry or physics and yet the discoverers had no thought of business possibilities when making their experiments and before their experiments proved successful no one in the business world would have dreamed of the enterprises that would grow from them. Though men have worked out the problems and other men have profited, no man arranged the matter. Of course there are cases where discoveries have been made at the demand of business necessity, but that was after the ground had been broken by some pioneer who had no thought of business. Although our civilization responds quickly to the leading of science no individual is in any sense a leader. It seems as if new discoveries are being made because they are needed in some plan that is over and above us. And in spite of all that has been accomplished each individual faces life and its problems as nakedly as those who lived before our systematized science was dreamed of.[44]

For McArthur, the split was not between the scientist and the humanist but between both and the materialist.

VII *Admonitions*

Although McArthur considered the city a great den of iniquity and the source of baneful influences, the rural world itself, he complained, had to shoulder some of the blame for its plight. If the city seemed a haven (if not a heaven) to defectors from the farm, it gained credence by comparison with the dreary existence of many in the country. They forever sat to meals of salt pork. McArthur prided himself on his table and suspected that the year-round routine of fried pork and potatoes broken only by "an occasional can of salmon," kept handy for an unsuspected visitor, or "a hen when the preacher calls" had a worse effect "than false economic doctrines or corrupt politics."[45] The young found little to entertain them in the country, for their games, like many of them, "had retreated to the city," a situation McArthur lamented with typical nostalgia. "Most of us," he wrote, "like to remember the homes of our childhood by the games we played in them and," he continued, "to have no games is to have fewer ties binding the children to the land. I am afraid the country is getting altogther too practical and joyless."[46]

If McArthur never directly blamed work for the exodus from the country, he knew how back-breaking and mind-deadening farming can be. Besides, he never pontificated on the moral value of hoeing (especially if the hands were blistered) and similar tasks associated with the "dignity" of manly labor. He

defended himself against idealizing farm life. "Work," he asserted, "is still a curse," and the milk pail, the bucksaw, and
the pitchfork, those devices that can make men drudges, might
well be its symbols. He was, of course, on the horns of a
dilemma. One of his strongest criticisms of city commerce was
that the farmer did all the hard work and that business got all
the profits. Yet he wished to persuade the "back-to-the lander"
of the attractiveness of country living. As a result he struck a
compromise. In the first place, he pointed out, muscle was not
the chief requirement in farming. The man of intelligence knew
that he got more for less labor from a small field than from a
larger one, if he fertilized the smaller property and sowed it
with good seed. In moderation, working with and among living
things could give an indefinable feeling of satisfaction and had
therapeutic value. Farming, correctly practiced, he listed among
the arts, for the farmer worked in accord with nature; he was
not "merely imitating it or describing it."

Farmers themselves were partly to blame for making their
work drudgery. They had become too busy trying to make
money to appreciate the beauty of the natural world. In "Why
I Stick to the Farm," McArthur had attempted to persuade
them of the opportunity that was theirs to live free of the
profit motive. They had made themselves slaves of the dollar,
not the soil, and McArthur, when aggrieved by their inattention,
did not hesitate to denounce those who had turned farming into
an agribusiness for their materialism as sharply as he denounced
businessmen for theirs. At times he saw the farmers as the true
betrayers of the cause, for they had remained on the land, but
had forsaken the faith of their fathers.

Most regrettably of all, the true significance of "home" was
being lost. Industry and perseverance directed away from the
ideal of homemaking to moneymaking took all pleasure from
work, for it no longer had any meaning as participation in the
natural processes for its own sake; no longer related to the
organic, it became mechanical and unimaginative. Not only had
the search for wealth made work a necessary evil, it had
destroyed the fabric of rural life. Home for some now was
merely a "speculation in real estate" and farming a matter of
acres owned, cost of production, and the "value of crops, stock,

and investment." For others home was simply a place to stay; a farm, an area of land, not a precious inheritance, and life, a negative affair—a dedication to "saving up." Even those farmers who just managed to make ends meet did not get off scot-free, despite McArthur's genuine sympathy for them. They frequently lacked pride in the land, also, and "their tumbled-down buildings and ragged fences ... were an injury to the whole countryside."[47] They did not accept the self-sufficiency that could have been theirs as it had been the pioneers'.

Farmers' lives whirled in vicious concentric circles of urban and rural. "City and country are now," he complains, "much alike in their devotion to money, power—in fact to all the root vices of the Seven Deadly Sins. The cities educate the country to extravagance, luxury, fashions and all their own follies so as to get a home market for the products that keep so great a part of labour employed. The country takes all this gladly and pays for it with food and raw materials."[48] According to the moderns, living like the pioneers (who knew "how to twiddle their thumbs") would be a waste of time, but one of these "moderns," Peter McArthur, liked to be able to say that "he farmed for his neighbours' amusement" and never ceased trying to convert farmers into devotees of the past. McArthur overlooked the fact of course that few could renounce the plow for the pen as an adjunct of livelihood.

McArthur never reduced life to a matter merely of food, shelter, and clothing, the certainties a farm could give, though he valued all these sincerely. He wished to persuade his readers that once these were assured one should relax and enjoy his leisure. Work, he charged, had become a bad habit among many, and he suggested that the Ontario Agriculture College needed a professor of leisure to teach its values on the farm. He wished there were more inconsequential people who liked sleighing "just for the fun of it" and fewer of the sobersided who, no longer alive to living, were wearing themselves out prematurely with incessant toil. One should take time to commune with nature and to read, to be sure not the modern historical romances, but pioneer history and the works of the old masters, and he even prescribed an annual rereading of *Plutarch's Lives, Gulliver's Travels, Robinson Crusoe*, and other great books.

Of course McArthur made his protest on behalf of leisure a club to belabor the city. The farmer should work to get his share of leisure, not to fill the coffers of the middleman with unearned profits, and should guard against an urban society that stole his leisure and then used it foolishly.

Every once in a while I see a paean in praise of work and I invariably set it down as the production of some toil-maniac of insufficient intellectual capacity to enable him to enjoy leisure. . . . If everyone did only the work needed to supply his own needs and used his leisure to develop the resources of his mind we would have a new world. . . . Those who have leisure under our present system do not know how to use it. Instead of developing themselves they degenerate through riotous excess. By having too much of other people's labour and none of their own they become parasites. . . . I am willing to do my share of work, but I want my share of leisure too, and I am not afraid of it. There is enough beauty in the world to enrich the leisure of any man.[49]

McArthur was committed to human values anywhere, not to the farming community alone; he believed that they had a greater chance of survival there than in the city, depersonalized as it was under the impact of profit-seeking, organization, and the machine. These were the evils that threatened the rural world and that it could avoid, if it wished. It had freedom and the necessities of life.

VIII   *"Back-to-the-Land"*

Convinced that the city was beyond redemption, McArthur made the salvation of the country his principal task before it, too, had been irreparably corrupted. He argued, he cajoled, he praised, he damned, he described, he narrated, reported, and dramatized, all in the name of persuading the farmer and the city-dweller alike to appreciate the richness of the simple life. His true hopes lay in the converts and the "prodigals": the urbanites who knew and disliked the city and those who knew and were homesick for the country. Both would recognize more readily and appreciate more fully than many of the stay-at-home farmers all that the simple life had to offer.

Openly proselytizing, he held forth as enticement the satisfaction that awaited all who abandoned an urban existence of "hurry and worry" and barren streets for a livelihood of peace, quietness, and neighborliness amid the beauty and vitality of the natural world. Unlike the coming of big business and the machine, such an intrusion would rejuvenate country life and establish homemaking as the core of its economy and culture. In this campaign of recruitment he pointed out, as he had to the restless farmers, that "living is of more account than even farming" (even scientific farming) and that newcomers "will learn how good it is to live ... free and independent."[50] Nor would they lack any of the worthwhile advantages of the metropolitan world, for the village was the heart of a farming community, not the center of Big Business organization. "The village stores and groceries," he informed the dreamers in the city (and the dissidents of the farm), "now sell fruits and delicacies that could be secured a few years ago only in the best city markets. There are churches and good schools everywhere and facilities for every reasonable enjoyment."[51] Progress deserved credit—as long as it knew when to stop.

Life in the country surpassed, or could surpass, life in the city, he told the back-to-the-landers, but it had its drawbacks, and, for all his gusto, McArthur warned that the farm was no place for greenhorns and dudes. The work required knowledge and training. The real farmers "enjoyed nothing more than the sight of 'a back-to-the-lander' in a tight box," and the "chance of profitably unloading farrow cows and wind-broken horses" on him."[52] Squirearchy had no place in McArthur's thinking either. It smacked too much of class distinction and Tory privilege. The back-to-the-lander "may flatter himself that he is the lord of the manor, but he finds that he is also the base scullion."[53] If he wanted a chicken for the pot he could call on no retainer but himself to prepare it. McArthur had been laughed at, but he had proved his philosophy and now stood ready as guide to the simple life with friendly tips and encouragement.

At first McArthur wished to persuade people of an ideal almost as much as to lead people literally back to the land. He did not wish others to try to live like him, but to accept his values. The history of the world, he theorized, could be written

in terms of the development of the home, and he did not think
that man had to go back to the country to find an ideal home,
nor did he have to return to pioneer ways. For McArthur, making a home meant putting it before moneymaking, and following
the pioneers meant largely the rejection of materialism as the
first value, and all that it gave rise to, for a kind of life that was
"unambitious" and neighborly. With the coming of World War
I, he began to stress the practical need for more people to
take up farming. Noting the drift from the rural areas, he proclaimed that not a house should remain vacant while the country was being stripped of its young men and at the very time
when it required more and more food for the allied armies. So
convinced was he that a world famine would soon come to pass
that he devised a program for greater production and informed
both Ottawa and Washington of it. So insistent had he become,
too, that people should "go farming" that he suggested "economic conscription," which would compel every young man
and woman of the farm to "spend, say three years in the production of the necessaries of life."[54]

From the hideousness of war, McArthur drew some comfort,
since it taught man the folly of his ways. "Mankind is going
'back to the land' as surely as day follows night," to establish
an order of "renewed strength and greater enlightenment."[55] For
a year or two following the war, when many returned men,
lured by government grants, tried farming, McArthur had high
hopes for the truth of his prophecy. These died shortly, for
the jazz age and the automobile age, not the return of innocence,
supplanted the years of struggle. The war had broken "the
earth hold of humanity"; society had become a thing of "gaudy
trappings," which closed its eyes to the age-old problems of
"food, clothing, and shelter." McArthur, his faith shaken not a
whit and true to his early religious training, warned these new
infidels that a day of wrath was at hand. In the name of the
"law of the acceleration of civilization" the downfall of New
York, Boston, Philadelphia and all the other world capitals
would come to pass, as would the disintegration of the farm
communities, no less accursed, "lusting" as they were for the
"modern conditions" that were hurrying the cities to their
destruction.[56]

A grim and cheerless vision, it heralded a brighter day, fortunately, "when man will be driven back" to the land by "cherubim with a flaming sword." Until that day should arrive, however, McArthur busied himself expounding less spectacular methods of saving the country and even of uniting it with the city so that both could live in peaceful coexistence. Once, on the basis that the two were alike, the country having prostituted itself to the city, he had argued that the difference both needed to bridge was between Civilization and Life, the latter meaning, of course, that something he found in nature. Now shining like a jewel, the city with its "wealth, luxury, education and culture [gave] all the things enlightened men and women desire . . . [and] the country [gave] safety and a sure existence."[57] The war revealed that all society had lost its earth hold and now needed a new footing on which both the rural and urban could stand together, a social hold incorporating all in one organized society. That social hold only life insurance could provide! In view of all the brickbats McArthur had flung at capitalism it appears a strange method of harmonizing the simple and the sophisticated life, but seems less so when placed in a context not so much of "the simple life" as of McArthur's social criticism.

IX *Man of Affairs*

Writing in "The World of Life," McArthur sets the simple life in its social and philosophical contexts:

The only wealth that interested me was the wealth of life and of being in accord with the infinite life by which I was surrounded. . . . Those who are in accord partake of life rather than of business prosperity. And at all times there is the healing of soul in being merged into that life without losing one's personality.

But the state of being in accord with the universal life is not constant. Civilization has its undoubted claims. Taxes must be paid—we must render unto Caesar. So from time to time the picture shifts and I am back in the world of men and facing the problems of civilization. At such times I take a roaring interest in politics, plan for better crops and bigger barns and discuss economic problems over the roadside fence with passing thinkers who are wrought up about such matters.[58]

Here McArthur touches on the two issues that plagued him almost to the end of his days. He recognized that to be viable the simple life could not close its eyes to social matters. It, more than the urban, needed to keep a close watch on political and economic affairs. There really was little ivory towerism in McArthur's philosophy; he never hesitated to engage in disputes about practicalities. He wished to find a political and economic foundation to match the philosophical.

Among the causes of some of his minor skirmishes was education. It is easy to misinterpret him here as a reactionary, for he attacked education. Yet it was not education in itself that roused his ire, but its lack of recognition of the interests of the rural world. It failed to interpret and relate to country life. McArthur wanted education to produce inner satisfaction and the desire to do rather than to get a better job. He recognized that the urban world had set up the curriculum and values of education, especially "getting on." Technical schools, he warned, may mean "turning out better servants for bigger and harder bosses."[59]

If McArthur took potshots at modern education, politics and business came constantly under his fire. "Since politics and economics are practically one," as he said,[60] he usually concerned himself with the effect of politics on rural economy rather than on rural philosophy. Moreover, since he always associated commerce and industry, which he disliked, with the Tories, an attack on one automatically meant an attack on the other.

Among the issues that were politico-economic, Reciprocity stirred him greatly, and soon after his return to Ekfrid he was arguing for it. Although not an out-and-out free-trader he looked on it as a propitious compromise and supported it in the federal election campaign of 1911, which resulted in an overwhelming defeat for the Liberal party. For McArthur the cause was not hard to find. It was obviously the work of big business protecting itself behind a tariff wall at the expense of the "common man." McArthur was writing when the opening of the West brought on a business boom in the East that weighted the economic balance of the country in favor of industry and commerce vis-à-vis agriculture. McArthur tended to see things as blacks and whites; so it was no problem to single out the businessman as the cause of all problems of the farming community. Before his rise to prominence, farmers had prospered. Now they found it harder to make a living, and by *post hoc propter hoc* reasoning McArthur had the answer.

Behind the public world of commerce lurked a little knot of bankers, whom McArthur criticized so vigorously that he feared the *Globe* and the *Farmer's Advocate* would suppress some of his articles during the time (1912), when the Bank Act was being revised.[61] McArthur had an out, however, and turned his magazine *Ourselves* into his mouthpiece. In it he makes clear how much of his antipathy derived from the normal thinking of frontier days, when the central bank seemed a great leech sucking the lifeblood of the rural area for the benefit of mergers and combines by which the country's finances were manipulated for the profit of the few. McArthur saw the branch bank system, though British in origin, as another of the dangers inherent in the modern drift toward centralization. It resulted in a shortage of money in rural areas so that they were being destroyed. Capitalism, as it had developed, had much to answer for.

The store in the village or town has not been allowed to grow, but has been crippled by the "system's" city department store; the factory has been absorbed by a merger and closed up or pushed to the wall by the system and is out of business; the town and village workmen praying for leave to toil, have had to follow the bank deposits to the big city. And yet when one looks down the dismal street of the deserted village he will see one gilded sign which was not there in the days of prosperity. Over the door of a once prosperous store, in big gold letters, read the sign of the branch bank."[62]

At the time, McArthur had a plan to cure the rural malaise through government control of the system:

If [The Minister of Finance] amended the bank act so as to give public government inspection it would spoil many a scheme of high finance which goes through now without any questions being asked. If he added an amendment restricting plans to any corporation or individual to ten per cent of the paid-up capital of the bank there would be no more of these eighteen million dollar loans; and if he made it the law, as it should be, that no director be allowed to borrow for himself or any business in which he is interested, any money from the bank of which he is a director, then we would find as directors of banks a different and better class of men. Then this set of greedy, cruel, grinding grafters would give place to men who would be real trustees for the people in collecting, investing and protecting their savings.[63]

The Minister, however, failed to act as suggested here, and McArthur had to wait another decade before finding a way around his problem of controlling freedom of enterprise without aid from the government.

Under the aegis of the "Big Interests" the cities fared no better than the rural districts, for directly or indirectly they turned labor into slavery because they themselves determined all by profit. "As John D. Rockefeller ... blandly informed the Senatorial Commission which was investigating his business methods: 'I am merely a clamourer for dividends.'" As regards the workers, they lived stultifying lives. What they did had "none of the charm it had for the old-time artisan who performed every operation himself," their machines symbolizing the heartlessness of the profit-seeker.[64]

As McArthur judged centralized finance—merger, trust, or combine—it worked against the farmer. Prices went up as local industry died away, and individual enterprise, as he understood it, lost its meaning. Discussing this phase of McArthur's stand against the "Lords of Finance" and the "Captains of Industry," F. W. Watt alludes to what he considers McArthur's inconsistency in attacking organizations on one hand and on the other defending "an egg-circle, a beef-ring ... or a labor union."[65] Yet McArthur is arguing here in terms of the old-fashioned bee. He distinguishes between a cooperation and an organization. The first provides a defense of the rights of the common man; the second, a weapon of attack for the few. One protected individualism; the other threatened to destroy it. Cooperation, according to McArthur, helped solve the problem of collectivism and free enterprise. It got rid of the middleman and put the producer and consumer on an equal footing. It was not an organization; it was not a benefit for the few at the expense of the many.

McArthur believed that the farmer could gain little redress through politics in an age of "big business and little government." Liberalism, he thought, stood for the ordinary citizen and greater Canadian autonomy. Yet the old-fashioned kind that "fought oppression and greed" had died after Laurier's defeat. Now Liberalism, too, represented centralized power. Though the Liberals wooed McArthur, he remained independent and refused to accept any nomination for office. Nor did he esteem the various farmers' movements highly. He does not discuss the Grange or the Patrons of Industry at all, but he wrote many times about the United Farmers of Ontario and praised the party for making the farmers' difficulties known. Yet he refused to join it, even when offered the position of leader by E. C. Drury, and finally came to oppose it altogether when it began "to invent new politics."[66] Moreover, it tended to focus the attention of the farmer on moneymaking. McArthur did suggest one plank—that they conscript the money made by the wartime profiteers.

X The Affable Stranger

McArthur summarized many of his views in *The Affable Stranger* (1920). He had stated them at various times previously, but here he brought them together. It was his social manifesto.[67] Again he warned against rugged individualism and mammonism even among the farmers. The book proposes the same old solutions, but with a difference. In the earlier books, he had preached "back-to-the-land" as a natural law. "The nationalisation of the land is immeasurably nearer than any one supposes," he stated, and continued in a manner typical of British empirical thinking as opposed to that of the theorists, "and it will be brought about by the blundering logic of events.... The work of education undertaken by Henry George and his disciples is now practically complete."[68] Ten years later the millenium seemed farther away than ever.

Like many other thinkers after World War I, McArthur examined what the various groups and "isms" had to offer. Capital had "organized business and established it in the great centres. When business was centralized, labor was centralized

and began to organize. Now capital and labor [were] at each
other's throats. . . ." Big unions fomented strikes, and so, too,
like Big Capital, "interfered with the rights of the majority of
people."[69] The farmers offered little more hope, since they also
were organizing for profit or political power.

As regards the modern economic theories of communism and
socialism, McArthur saw nothing good in them. Some readers
assume him to have been left wing because of his onslaught
on capitalism, forgetting that the remedy proposed, not the
problem, determines such categories. He wanted a return to
old values, not "wild new politics." In "Prince Kropotkin's Cow,"
he derides communism as foolish and impractical. "Back to the
Primitive" attacks socialism as the philosophy of the Lotus-
Eaters because of the socialists' "aversion to old-fashioned work."

Yet "a majority will be saved." Despite the rise of the city and
the defection of the farmers from the pioneer tradition, he foresaw the day when the cities would rot away and "hunger and
fear" would force mankind to return to the old ideals and the
truly democratic again. In a less cosmic perspective he found
reason for hope in the reaction of the city-dwellers to the strikes
of the time in Winnipeg, Seattle, and elsewhere. Their citizens
"made it quite clear that the big, quaking foolish majority is no
longer in the mood to put up with the tyranny of noisy minor-
ities."[70] Ever an optimist, McArthur argued that "a majority
will be saved" on the basis also of his faith that the Soul of man
will win out against Chaos. Brotherhood only "waits for leader-
ship." And he quotes Gustave Le Bon as the authority for the
belief that the will of the majority is final in a world where
man, "blundering, rebellious of divine control, [is] forever struggling upward."[71]

There is a lot of fuzzy and wishful thinking in McArthur's
arguments, and the best he can do is promise that the "future
may have trouble in store for the profiteers, agitators, bureau-
crats, and others who are wailing that the world is going to the
devil. . . ."[72] These were people whom the war had spawned
and who now threatened to undo what good had come from that
bloodbath. As yet, however, McArthur had failed to describe
the methods by which man could rid himself of this kind of
enemy and create a new society.

Watt makes the point that by 1920 it was no longer possible to see an Eden in the Canadian rural scene. Actually, McArthur had never tried to see one; he had a farm, not a garden, in mind in setting up his ideal state and might well have accepted the nineteenth-century English slogan "two acres and a cow" as in general expressing his central concept. McArthur believed that agrarianism, not Arcadianism, was the Canadian tradition, and in *The Affable Stranger* he makes a strong case for the need to revere it. As an ardent nationalist he aimed at wakening modern Canadians to their natural heritage. They did not need to bow to modern "isms" or to other nations. They only needed to see that they inherited the spirit of true democracy and the hardiness of the pioneers. Moreover, with this background Canada should stand as "a free nation within the Empire."

When in London, McArthur had published "An Ode of Empire," in which he wrote as a colonial celebrating the British tradition, but on returning to Ekfrid he had almost immediately composed a song expressing his deep love of Canada.[73] *The Affable Stranger* takes up the subject of "Loyalty," but defines it as being true to ourselves. His colonialism had not developed into "Imperialism." Canadians had the mythology to unite their regions into a nation without destroying their identities. What was required was personal action in the name of humanistic and democratic values. Nationalism was a matter of character, not of legislation.

World War I had done much to foster McArthur's nationalism. He had organized the Greater Production Committee to focus the attention of the country as a whole on its duty to its own people and its allies. Canadians needed "loyalties beyond their own country" to become a nation. He stood with Laurier against national conscription if it did not take into consideration the needs and nature of various classes and regions, and he refused to question the loyalty of the French-Canadians. Above all, a country founded by "humble people" had shown its mettle on European battlefields, so taking a long step toward the greater self-government he deemed the country's right.

If McArthur believed that Canada should guard against British domination, he is equally explicit that she be aware of the role of the United States in Canadian affairs. In his articles on Reciprocity he had commented on the problems inherent in the expansion of American business into Canada and had warned that the country, without control of her economy, would have no real control over her destiny. Yet he was pro-Canadian, not anti-American, and, as the title *The Affable Stranger* suggests, he wanted Canada to adopt an independent yet friendly attitude toward the United States and to avoid prejudicial judgments of her great neighbor.

XI   The Last Law—Brotherhood

Although *The Affable Stranger* expresses the belief that Canada possesses the qualities to form a strong nation, with no need to stand in awe of the United States, to bow to Imperialism, or to adopt "new politics," the book does little more than express belief. *The Last Law—Brotherhood*, however, explains the means by which this belief can be acted on. Thanks to life insurance the country could have democratic, or people's, capitalism. Canadians had long had a say in the politics of the land; now they could have the same privilege with regard to its economics. They could take out insurance policies. Insurance companies invest in large enterprises and therefore could establish a people's ownership of them. In this way insurance provided all the advantages of public ownership without stifling private initiative. Besides, life insurance protected the family and the home. Moreover, the farmers could remain independent. They had from the first accepted the idea of cooperation and should look on insurance as a cooperative venture. Insurance funds would be at their service to buy land; the common man could "become a part of the social organization which now supports humanity as it was once supported by the land. Indeed, in this way [he] could even secure a hold on the land for much of the most valuable land is now mortgaged to the great insurance companies."[74]

McArthur realized that in his praise of the insurance companies he was backtracking. In *Ourselves,* he had stated that less than a dozen men "control the income of all the larger insurance companies and their allies."[75] He knew also that the farmers thought he had "been bought out by the Big Interests." To bolster his case he went to the Bible to prove that Brotherhood is a law of human society and, among the moderns, called on Condorcet and Gustave Le Bon to support him. Even "the ruthless bolshevick" accepted Brotherhood as law, but the proletariat "in trying to divide wealth . . . would destroy it."[76] Life insurance did not destroy but shared wealth.

Despite the discrepancies between the earlier and later comments that McArthur made about insurance, he had finally convinced himself that it reconciled big and little capital and made private enterprise responsible to the public. Through insurance the common man gained the benefits of socialism without its drawbacks, for the government could not interfere with the rights of the individual. Whatever the flaws in reasoning here, one thing is obvious. The social and economic theories presented in McArthur's last book were aimed at preserving the values and the way of life that had inspired almost everything else he wrote.

XII *A Triumph for Tradition*

For all McArthur's literary ambitions, for all his politics and economic theories, for all his doubts and inconsistencies, the real McArthur was the McArthur who lived the simple life at Ekfrid (1908–1924) after his return from the United States. It became the rock on which he founded his nationalism and his faith. It subsumed his concept of the kinship of nature and broadened out until it finally equated the simple and the good life.

McArthur knew that in looking backward, his favorite perspective, he could find many early apostles of the faith. Whitman and Thoreau, and even Virgil, had taken similar stands, although Thoreau slighted the human and stressed the metaphysical more than the others did. McArthur found support also in Wordsworth, not only in his nature poems but more significantly in *The Excursion*.[77] William Cobbett was another who McArthur knew had upheld the agrarian tradition as a social ideal, convinced that man is happiest when living in the country and dependent only on himself and nature. McArthur could and did go back to Genesis for final verification of the simple life, for he held no faith in a heavenly city, Biblical or not. Yet there is little Arcadianism in McArthur's books, for their philosophy derives from the Old Testament world of the Patriarchs, where one earned his bread by the sweat of his brow tending flocks or laboring in the vineyards, knowing nothing of the delights of reverie or of lotus-land indolence.

McArthur owes much of his enthusiasm for agrarianism to his own experiences. As a young man of twenty he had followed the tradition of the time and had taken the high road to the city where, he dreamed, success awaited him. In this evolution from innocence to experience he tried to conform to the standards of a world which "men have developed for themselves and which they describe as progress and civilization."[78] He even went so far in *The Sufficient Life* as to disparage the devotee of the simple life as "a nuisance to himself and to everyone with whom he comes in contact," and, he continued, "those who choose the simple life are not missed from the great sane multitude that is doing the world's work."[79] Despite this slight, McArthur harbored a genuine love of the bucolic. He had lived too long on a farm to be able to forget it. Not until his years in London, however, did he seriously consider returning to it, confiding to Vaux that he was now as eager to get back to the farm as he had been to leave it. Yet it would be untrue to think of him as the prodigal he depicts in the sonnet "The Prodigal," for he remained in the city after his return from London and probably would never have gone back to the farm had his advertising agency in New York not collapsed in the depression of 1906. Though one might question the love of farm life as McArthur's prime motive for abandoning the city and argue that in the early essays on the delights and benefits of the simple life McArthur rationalized his own failure as an urbanite, it is not possible to deny that he became a sincere convert to the faith, nor that, as is usual with converts, he became a zealous missionary for the cause, for a life lived according to agrarian idealism.

Of the many facets of agrarianism that McArthur examined, the most significant related to the dynamic environment, not as something to be observed in formal nature study or communed with in meditation, but as something that permitted him to live in accord with nature and to participate in processes. God was the Great Partner, and the farmer, the true artist. While others worked with words and colors and sounds he worked with life itself, and his occupation moreover offered him "possibilities of spiritual and mental culture beyond any other."[80] On another level man working in harmony with nature had no need to trouble about the "nightmare of human affairs," for he had the essentials of food and shelter ready to hand, a benefit of the simple life that McArthur emphasized during his first years at Ekfrid. He saw the farm then as a haven and refuge, a place of peace and safety for one hurled back penniless by the world's metropolises.

Proof positive of the merit and practicability of agrarianism, McArthur believed, could be found not only in accounts of societies of the distant past but also in the story of the men and women who had made their homes in the wilderness of Ontario a few short decades before, and even during his own childhood. McArthur revered the pioneers and long before social history (and certainly Canadian social history) had been generally accepted as important history, he had become an advocate of its study. "The history of Canada has never been written because it is so simple and wonderful," he declared. "The glory of Canada does not rest on the history of soldiers and statesmen . . . but on the still unwritten unsung story of the pioneers."[81]

McArthur himself, though he disclaimed any ability as historian, did write a history, if not of Canada at least of Ontario, when all his essays on the early settlers are taken together. By describing life on his farm he was writing it, since he made the pioneers his models, and his books are a case history of the simple life, which he generally equated with their way of life, not "adventures in contentment" like David Grayson's, not struggles to drive life into a corner like Thoreau's. McArthur was too robust a man to write as Grayson and too fond of rural society to write as Thoreau. He lived for years in a log house that had neither electric lights nor a telephone in it. In season he dined on mushrooms, puffballs, wild berries, and often, especially during his first years at Ekfrid, sat down to roast rabbit for his main dish. Always at hand was the produce of his farm—apples, plums, and garden vegetables, milk, butter, eggs, chickens (and occasionally a plump turkey or duck). He traveled by horse and buggy, made maple syrup and apple butter, husked corn, cut and split his winter's wood, stored apples in an apple pit, "salted down" pork against future want. In many respects, of course, he lived like other farmers of his time, but with this difference: he did not plan to build a fine new home, buy an automobile, or "go in for" cash crops.

McArthur drew on pioneer history not only for his mode of living but for many of his essays. Sometimes he merely alludes to it in passing. "We," he notes by way of comparison with the early settlers, "wear finely laundered linen when we go to town, instead of donning paper collars and putting butter on our hair."[82] Or he remembers the log houses of old with their open fireplaces and their dooryard flower beds, which he preferred to all others, for "not even the fabled 'Beds of amaranth and moly / Where soft winds lull us breathing lowly,' can surpass a Canadian garden brimming with the old-fashioned flowers beloved of childhood."[83] Sometimes his asides say much succinctly about early farming with their remarks on cattle that got "through the winters by eating buds and licking moss off the trees," and sheep of "the pioneer variety that were half goat and half greyhound."[84] Sprinkled through his books, too, are lengthy commentaries on social life. He describes Sunday school picnics, which were, of course, much better "then"; fall fairs, which were much better "then" and where one could enjoy horse races or that popular contest that set competitors to catch a greased pig; winter evenings spent whittling baskets from peach stones—the knives were better "then"; barn-raising bees when the settlers joined to do a neighbor a good turn; a visit from an Indian peddler with his "baskets, axe-handles, whipstocks, and bead-work pincushions," or, even better, a visit to his wigwam with its bows and arrows, "an event in the life of a small boy."[85]

Other essays read like a history of pioneering farming: cutting, logging, and burning trees, sickling, or cradling, grain; curing it in shocks of ten or thirteen sheaves and threshing it with a flail or a horse-powered threshing machine. Others tell of cocking or stacking hay, early beekeeping, and one describes that remarkable annual event of pioneer Western Ontario, the autumnal turkey roundup.[86] There is the additional fact that many of his discussions of contemporary life have now themselves become social history, for his days of pitchfork, crosscut saw, and buggy have faded into the past. Occasionally, too, he pictures the countryside of early nineteenth-century Ontario, as in his visit to the Talbot settlement, or records farm reaction to the coming of the automobile, and once writes excitedly about the first airship to fly over his beloved Ekfrid township.

The heroes of pioneer history were not soldiers and statesmen; they were cast in a greater mold. "God-compelled and God-led as were the Israelites," they held to the old codes of thought that "man's earthhold was his greatest treasure."[87] They had tried "the new experiment in civilization . . . which made the home rather than money the unit of success."[88] Although much in these eulogies is rhetorical, the theme of McArthur's social history is very clear in them, for they stress the point that the settlers had put the establishment of a home above all else and had made their way of living their way of making a living.

Typical of much thinking in pioneer social history, he attributes the growth of democracy to frontier farm life. With the passing of time he saw, or thought he saw, the farm as a place of refuge become the farm as a place where one could enjoy the greatest right of all, "the right of being independent," and that this freedom had given rise to a society where all were on an equal footing. The pioneers had succeeded because of their egalitarianism, as the bee symbolized, on the one hand, and their self-dependence on the other—because of their industry, thrift, frugality, and perseverance. These were values that McArthur admired and tried to instill into his readers together with a warning of the dangers to the nation if the concept of success changed from making homes to making fortunes because of all the divisive and depersonalizing effects that that goal would entail. McArthur's emphasis on home sweet home has something Victorian about it, and in that way is a reflection of an age when the peoples of Europe made a mass exodus to the new worlds. It has overtones, also, of his personal experiences when he had beaten from pillar to post trying to make his own home in the inimical environment of great cities.

McArthur's philosophy of history and of nature are cut from the same cloth. As man, like Antaeus, is powerless unless rooted in nature, so is he powerless if not rooted in history. McArthur knew that the great achievement of settling Canada, of turning it from forest to farm, had established agrarianism as the tradition of the nation. He feared that in the name of progress and urbanization the people would neglect their history without even learning its facts or acknowledging its importance; hence he had set himself the task of teaching them both. For him the pioneers established the goal of his "great Canadian dream." Progress paradoxically meant a return to the past. To disregard the early settlers and their ideals. was for the nation to run the risk of losing purpose and direction. McArthur may not have realized the difficulty of finding a satisfactory common tradition for the "two Canadas," but he saw clearly the need of one for a new land and certainly for Canada if she was to have a national identity.

In recent years the kind of past McArthur depicted has been labeled as myth (the agrarian myth), largely on the basis of the belief that farms stultify and that the uneducated is the uncouth, that nostalgia blurs the vision. Critics say pioneer life, far from being ideal, was one of joyless isolation or a struggle for survival. These are modern views, largely urban and essentially Tory. They belong to the aristocratic tradition of early immigrant English gentle ladies, not to the Scottish liberal tradition of William "Tiger" Dunlop and his like to which McArthur belonged.

The pioneer world was no heaven, and the pioneers were no angels. McArthur knew these facts and never hesitated to include them in his commentaries. His was not blind ancestor worship. In his pioneer world in the springtime, the roads became quagmires, the streams impassable rivers, and the farmlands often little more than swamps. There, too, the work was laborious in the extreme. Food was sometimes scarce and the menu often catch as catch can with frumentary (boiled wheat) as cereal, "braxie" and oatmeal as staples, and dried apples as dessert—those products of the paring bee, which as they shriveled as apple beads or on an apple screen, became " 'a murmurous haunt of flies' " and "a substitute for food. . . ."[89] Mc-

Arthur knew that some pioneers were usurers and some, skin-flints.[90] All laid waste the forests and wildlife without misgiving. He recognized the materialism of many of their values and preached a religion based on a love of nature, not a fear of God, as a safeguard against the one and a substitute for the other.

What McArthur wished to make clear, vis-à-vis those who attack agrarianism as a sentimental myth, was that the pioneers lived positively. Many were rough-and-ready adventurers accustomed to hardship and toil from childhood, and the majority looked on their homesteads as the first chance to make their own way free from suppression and class privilege. Far better the so-called terror of New World forests than the fears of Old World rural enclosure or city unemployment (or even employment in early-nineteenth-century factories). Even if the forest were an enemy, the settler knew that against it he had a fair chance of winning, not so much in a struggle for survival as in a battle to make his life prevail, not as the "self-made man," the glory of the Victorian doctrine of "self-help," but as an independent human being, his scale of success measured in terms of neighborliness and bountiful harvests. More than anything else, however, McArthur tried to demonstrate by example and convince by argument and description that life on a farm with its work, variety, and vitality could satisfy any who remained true to the ideals of agrarianism.

Since the days when McArthur made his stand for these ideals, much has changed. His old house in Ekfrid township is gone, and the barnyard is deserted. The *Farmer's Advocate* has ceased publication; the *Globe*, in which he once proclaimed the Grit and the farmers' cause, has long since wedded the *Mail and Empire*, and years ago gave over such features as McArthur's columns and "The Farmer's Page." His rural philosophy has fewer adherents, and the family farm is dying under the baneful impact of concrete, urban sprawl, and agribusiness.

In one sense, and a very real sense, however, nothing has changed, for McArthur's work keeps fresh the palmy days when Fenceviewer, " 'that serpent of old Nile,' " the old gobbler, the "Prussian" of the farmyard, and Socrates, the bellicose goat, "held the world in awe." McArthur's pages live, too, as tributes to the fascination of wild creatures and their world of field and woodlot. Now whimsical, McArthur writes a remarkably original essay about a mockingbird; now nostalgic, a moving commentary about the trees that stood about his boyhood home; now pensive, a beautifully sensitive appreciation of the "solitude of rain." Like a great prism his nature essays reflect the lights and shadows of the world of the senses and, like delicate antennae, catch murmurs of some meaning that lies beyond.

Finally, McArthur also records the responses of a man of singular sensibility and of a writer of notable talent to the effect of modernism on the old Canadian tradition stemming from the values and achievements of the early settlers. If McArthur's life reflects and manifests something of the vitality and purport of that tradition, his writing, with its compelling imaginative sympathy and broad understanding of the world from which it derives, makes the tradition even more significant, establishing and revealing it as a vital truth in our literature and culture. As his essays show nature as a road to peace and spirituality, they also turn pioneer days into living history and celebrate the rural way of life as a road to true self-fulfillment and its ideals as the bases on which nationhood must take its stand.

Notes and References

Queen's University, Kingston, Ontario, and the University of New Brunswick have McArthur letters, but the great bulk of his papers is housed at the University of Western Ontario at London. Unless otherwise stated, all references to letters are to those in the library there.

Introduction

1. Peter McArthur's mother (1817–1902) came from Lochalsh, and his father (1809–1884), from Shipness. The McArthurs belonged to the Old Free Kirk.

2. The log house (32' x 23') that Peter McArthur (the father) built in 1854 has been preserved at Doon, in the Western Ontario Village.

3. McArthur married on the strength of his position with *Truth*. He received a salary of one hundred dollars a week. Daniel is the son referred to.

4. McArthur had barely arrived in New York before he found himself in "a state of violent collaboration with Nelson Wheatcroft on a four-act comedy dama," but it has remained "work in progress." With *Truth* he acted as drama critic, but did not try writing plays again until he went to Amityville. There he wrote a blank verse tragedy, *Prince Aguilar*, supposedly in the Shakespearean manner. No one would stage it or publish it, but he did manage to salvage three poems from it for *The Prodigal and Other Poems*—an elegy "To D. A. McKellar" (the dedicatory sonnet of *Prince Aguilar*) and "Dolce Far Niente" and "Man," both of which suggest that life means nothing and that reverie and indolence are the only satisfactory ways of living, a conclusion strangely at odds with the theme of the sonnets. *The Priest of Amen-Ra*, an incomplete closet drama, followed shortly. Like the sonnets, it centered on a man who had sinned but who had returned to service beyond what "foolish priests imposed," for he had learned that God "knows no worship save in work well done" according to His will. Words have their place, nevertheless, for through them the Voice gives the good man the right and power to teach others how they may do worthy acts. The play is very serious but scarcely tragic or dramatic.

At Amityville, McArthur wrote and played in a romantic comedy, *Love Lends a Hand*. Although a thing of stock characters and situations, it pleased the audience according to the *Signal* of Babylon, but the play went no further than the local theater. Undaunted, McArthur wrote a play for children, *Peter Piper*, but it was never played. It is a clever tour de force and demonstrates McArthur's ability with light verse. With this piece, McArthur closed his career as playwright, except for the chaotic verse drama "The Unknown Soldier," which he was working on when he died.

Chapter One

1. "Our Poets," the *Globe*, February 5, 1916, p. 17.
2. *Ibid.*
3. *Around Home*, p. 71.
4. *The Red Cow*, p. 284.
5. Letter to Vaux, July 22, 1924.
6. "On Having Known a Poet," *Atlantic Monthly*, 97 (May, 1906), p. 712.
7. *Friendly Acres*, p. 36.
8. Report of an interview with Jay Hambidge in an undated and unidentified newspaper clipping among the McArthur papers in the library at the University of Western Ontario. Date probably January, 1924.
9. *In Pastures Green*, p. 71.
10. *Ibid.*, p. 83.
11. "Duty," *The Prodigal and Other Poems*, p. 19.
12. "Prefatory," *Lines*, p. [3].
13. "Your Holiday," the *Globe*, May 6, 1911, p. 13.
14. "The Prodigal," *The Prodigal and Other Poems*, p. 13.
15. "Consecration," *ibid.*, p. 23.
16. "Earthborn," *ibid.*, p. 16. The poem is entitled "Autochthon" in *Lines*, p. 6.
17. "The True Evangel," *The Prodigal and Other Poems*, p. 7.
18. "Life," *ibid.*, p. 15.
19. "Summum Bonum," *ibid.*, p. 27.
20. "The Ocean Liner," *ibid.*, p. 32.
21. "Sugar Weather," *ibid.*, p. 35.
22. "Spring, Spring, Spring!" the *Globe*, April 17, 1915, p. 13.
23. *In Pastures Green*, p. 222.
24. "The Home Dream," *Around Home*, p. 245.
25. "Walt Whitman and Cosmic Consciousness," an undated manuscript among the McArthur papers at the University of West-

ern Ontario. McArthur here writes of *Cosmic Consciousness* (1901), by Richard Maurice Bucke, and argues, vis-à-vis Bucke, that the power by which man can catch a glimpse of the meaning of the universe is possessed by all men from the lowest to the highest. McArthur disliked the elitism of Bucke's theory of genius and considered it a misreading of Whitman's significance as a poet of the people.

26. *Ibid.*, p. 14.

27. The manuscript is in the library at the University of Western Ontario.

28. "Last winter I made up two plays from Walt Whitman's poems to be put on the movies, the poems to be chanted from a phonograph while the pictures are being shown. . . . Kennerly, who owns the Whitman copyrights, . . . accepted them and I am . . . to superintend the staging. . . ." Letter to Vaux, October 4, 1914.

"I am . . . waiting to hear from Kennerly about the moving picture shows, but I am afraid I delayed matters by declining to go to New York when he wanted me." Letter to Vaux, December 21, 1914. Undoubtedly influenced by the war then being waged, McArthur selected his readings from "Drum-Taps."

29. F. W. Watt, "Peter McArthur and the Agrarian Myth," *Queen's Quarterly*, 67, 2 (Summer, 1960), pp. 246, 247.

30. "To the Birds," *The Prodigal and Other Poems*, p. 50.

31. "A Parent's Plea," *ibid.*, p. 34.

32. "To My Fashionable Fiancée," *ibid.*, p. 55.

33. "In Oblivion," *ibid.*, p. 49.

34. "Tutankhamen," the *Globe*, February 7, 1923, p. 4.

35. "A Crane Song," the *Globe*, March 26, 1924, p. 4. (*The Best of Peter McArthur* [Toronto: Clarke, Irwin & Company, 1967], p. 171.)

36. "The Mocking Bird," *Around Home*, p. 109.

Chapter Two

1. William Arthur Deacon, manuscript of an address given to the Canadian Authors' Club, Toronto, 1924, p. 13. McArthur papers, the University of Western Ontario.

2. McArthur diary. McArthur papers, the University of Western Ontario.

3. The *Canadian Magazine*, XXXV, 5 (September, 1910), p. 432.

4. *Truth*, XV, 490 (September 5, 1896), pp. 10–11.

5. "The Row in the North Riding," *Ourselves*, I, 2 (November, 1910), p. 60.

6. *Ibid.*, p. 59.

7. *Ourselves,* I, 4 (January, 1911), pp. 184–187. (*The Best of Peter McArthur,* pp. 235–237.)

8. "The Over-looking of Gideon," *Canadian Magazine,* XXXVI, 2 (December, 1910), pp. 144, 146.

9. "Baldy McSporran," the *Globe,* October 28, 1911, p. 21. (*The Best of Peter McArthur,* p. 213.)

10. "A Farm Fable," the *Globe,* July 11, 1919, p. 4.

11. Letter to Vaux, December 13, 1897.

12. Letter to Vaux, December 26, 1897.

13. *Ibid.*

14. Manuscript of speech entitled "Hyphenated Canadianism," p. 1. McArthur papers, the University of Western Ontario.

Chapter Three

1. Letter to Vaux, December 13, 1897.

2. Letter to Vaux, October 23, 1903.

3. *Truth,* XIV, 437 (August 31, 1895), p. 2.

4. H. Addington Bruce, "Hard Knocks for an Optimist," *London Free Press,* December 3, 1966, p. 6M.

5. *Truth,* XVI, 528 (May 27, 1897), p. 7.

6. The *Gazette* (Montreal). Undated reference, McArthur papers.

7. Letter from Hambidge to McArthur, July, 1902. McArthur papers, the University of Western Ontario.

8. Letter to Mrs. McArthur, September 3, 1902.

9. Letter to Vaux, October 15, 1902.

10. Letter to Vaux, October 28, 1902.

11. Letter to Mrs. McArthur, September 25, 1902.

12. Letter to Vaux, October 2, 1902.

13. Letter to Vaux, October 28, 1902.

14. Letter to Vaux, October 8, 1911.

15. "The Monthly Talk," *Ourselves,* I, 1 (October, 1910), p. 1.

16. *Ourselves,* I, 1 (October, 1910), facing p. 1.

Chapter Four

1. Peter McArthur, "What men they were," *In Pastures Green,* p. 48. See "Jimmy Once," *Farmer's Advocate* (January 5, 1922), p. 11.

2. *Sir Wilfrid Laurier,* pp. 93–94.

3. "Who's Who," *Ourselves,* I, 4 (January, 1911), p. 153.

4. "Sir Wilfrid Laurier," *ibid.,* pp. 155, 156–157.

5. E. C. Drury, *Farmer Premier* (Toronto: McClelland and Stewart, 1966), pp. 61–62.

6. Letter (undated) to Daniel McArthur.

7. *Sir Wilfrid Laurier*, pp. 34–35.

8. Letter to Vaux, February 13, 1920.

9. A. H. Colquhuon, review of *Sir Wilfrid Laurier*, in the *Canadian Historical Review*, I, 1 (March, 1920), pp. 86–87.

10. *Sir Wilfrid Laurier*, p. 170.

11. *Ibid.*, pp. 72–76.

12. Letter to Vaux, September 8, 1923.

13. *Sir Wilfrid Laurier*, p. 89.

14. McArthur's defense of the Liberals and attack on the Tories runs from p. 122 to p. 146.

15. *Around Home*, pp. 191–192. *In Pastures Green*, pp. 125–127.

16. *Ourselves*, I, 2 (November, 1910), p. 81.

17. *Ibid.*, p. 77.

18. The *Globe*, July 17, 1909, p. 17.

19. *Cayuga Brook*, p. 103. McArthur papers, the University of Western Ontario. McArthur discusses intellectual snobbery in Canadian literature at some length in the *Globe*, February 8, 1913, p. 15.

20. The *Globe*, December 4, 1920, p. 4.

21. *The Affable Stranger*, p. 52. McArthur, always a stickler for old-time ways, attacks the movies in this chapter also on the grounds of their commercialism and the deleterious effect of American propaganda on Canada.

22. *Stephen Leacock*, p. 136.

23. *To Be Taken With Salt*, pp. 65, 114–115.

24. The *Globe*, September 4, 1920, p. 27.

25. *To Be Taken With Salt*, p. 154.

26. *In Pastures Green*, pp. 200–201.

27. "Romance," the *Globe*, January 8, 1920, p. 13.

28. *Ibid.*

29. *Stephen Leacock*, pp. 138–139, 147.

30. *Ibid.*, pp. 161–162.

31. "Introduction," *Sunshine Sketches of a Little Town*, ed. Malcolm Ross (Toronto: McClelland and Stewart, 1960), p. ix.

32. Robertson Davies, *Stephen Leacock* (Toronto: McClelland and Stewart, 1970), p. 55.

33. Letter from Lorne Pierce to McArthur, January 2, 1923.

34. Letter from Leacock to McArthur, February 1, 1923.

35. Letter from McArthur to Leacock, May 25, 1923.

36. Letter from Pierce to McArthur, June 6, 1923.

37. Letter from Leacock to McArthur, July 16, 1923.

38. Letter from McArthur to Pierce, January 24, 1923.

39. "Greater Toronto," the *Globe*, May 17, 1924, p. 4. (*The Best of Peter McArthur*, p. 240.)

40. McArthur, *Stephen Leacock*, pp. 133, 149.

41. *Ibid.*, pp. 134–135.

42. *Ibid.*, pp. 143, 128, 129.

43. Donald Cameron, *Faces of Leacock* (Toronto: Ryerson Press, 1967), p. 172.

44. McArthur, *Stephen Leacock*, p. 133.

45. McArthur papers, the University of Western Ontario.

46. "The Prodigal," *The Prodigal and Other Poems*, p. 13.

47. McArthur, *Stephen Leacock*, p. 143.

48. *Ibid.*, p. 144.

49. *Ibid.*, pp. 159–160.

50. *Ibid.*, pp. 149–150.

Chapter Five

1. Letter from McArthur to Duncan McKellar, September 27, 1887. McKellar (1865–1899) was for years McArthur's closest friend. From 1888 to 1890, McKellar was assistant editor, drama critic, and illustrator of *Saturday Night*. In the early 1890's he went to New York and again established his name as a magazine illustrator. Ill health, however, forced him to give up his work and return to his home in Penetanguishene, where he died a youthful victim of consumption. Many of his brilliant letters to McArthur are preserved among the McArthur papers at the University of Western Ontario. McArthur was instrumental in having McKellar's poetry published in a volume entitled simply *Poems* (Toronto: Thomas Allen, 1922).

2. Kenneth Wells, "Introduction" to *In Pastures Green*, p. xi.

3. Letter to Vaux, December 1, 1912.

4. Letter to Vaux, October 13, 1913.

5. Letter to Daniel McArthur, September 9, 1917.

6. *Cayuga Brook*, pp. 103–104.

7. *In Pastures Green*, p. 201.

8. *Ibid.*, p. ix.

9. Letter to Daniel McArthur, December 9, 1917.

10. "Home News," the *Globe*, October 16, 1916, p. 6. (*The Best of Peter McArthur*, p. 66.)

11. *Friendly Acres*, p. 192.

12. "Peter McArthur," *Daily Sentinel-Review* (Woodstock, Ontario), October 30, 1924, p. 2.

13. McArthur papers, the University of Western Ontario.

14. "Quotations," the *Globe*, September 8, 1920, p. 6.

15. *Around Home*, p. 27.

16. *Ibid.*, p. 44.

17. *In Pastures Green*, p. 111.

18. *Ibid.*, p. 95.

19. William Arthur Deacon, *Peter McArthur*, p. 137.

20. William Arthur Deacon, manuscript of address given to the Canadian Authors' Club, Toronto, 1924, p. 13. McArthur papers, the University of Western Ontario.

21. William Arthur Deacon, *Peter McArthur*, p. 133.

22. Kenneth Wells, "Introduction" to *In Pastures Green*, p. ix.

23. *In Pastures Green*, pp. 125–128.

24. *The Red Cow*, p. 97.

25. *Friendly Acres*, p. 57.

26. *In Pastures Green*, p. 124.

27. Letter to Vaux, September 1, 1910.

28. Brandon Conron, "Essays, 1880–1920," *Literary History of Canada*, ed. C. Klinck et al. (Toronto: University of Toronto Press, 1965), p. 345.

29. *Ibid.*

30. *In Pastures Green*, p. 351.

31. *The Red Cow*, p. 98.

32. *In Pastures Green*, p. 189.

33. *Around Home*, p. 77.

Chapter Six

1. McArthur papers, the University of Western Ontario.

2. McArthur, *Stephen Leacock*, p. 158.

3. *Friendly Acres*, pp. 189, 191.

4. Letter to author from William Arthur Deacon, June 25, 1964.

5. Letter to author from Daniel McArthur, July 5, 1964.

6. *To Be Taken With Salt*. These three epigrams are found on pages 157, 152, and 156–157 in order as given in this text.

7. *Ibid.*, p. 157.

8. *Ibid.*, p. 166.

9. *Ibid.*, pp. 19–20.

10. *Ibid.*, pp. 12–16.

11. *Ibid.*, p. 110.

12. *Ibid.*, p. 103.

13. McArthur, *Stephen Leacock*, p. 128.

14. *To Be Taken With Salt*, p. 80.

15. *Ibid.*, pp. 80–81.

16. Letter to Vaux, December 21, 1903.

17. *In Pastures Green*, p. 30.

18. *Ibid.*, p. 167.

19. *Ibid.*, pp. 118, 170, 320.

20. "Essays 1880–1920," *Literary History of Canada*, p. 344.

21. *In Pastures Green*, p. 135.

22. *Ibid.*, p. 43.

23. "A Reminiscence," the *Globe*, June 30, 1917, p. 12. In the same paper, April 12, 1913, p. 15, he resents being thought only a humorist.

24. *In Pastures Green*, pp. 11–12.

25. *The Red Cow*, p. 39.

26. *Ibid.*, p. 152.

27. *In Pastures Green*, pp. 4–5.

28. *Friendly Acres*, p. 93.

29. *Truth*, XVI, 535 (July 17, 1897), pp. 10–11.

30. *In Pastures Green*, p. 254.

31. *Around Home*, p. 236.

32. *Friendly Acres*, p. 141.

33. *Around Home*, p. 222.

34. *The Red Cow*, p. 243.

35. *Around Home*, pp. 129–130.

36. *Friendly Acres*, p. 193.

Chapter Seven

1. *Around Home*, p. 82.

2. *In Pastures Green*, p. 188.

3. *Ibid.*, p. 141.

4. *Ibid.*, p. 317.

5. *Ibid.*, p. 121.

6. *Ibid.*, pp. 146–147. See also the *Globe*, June 3, 1911, p. 15. (*The Best of Peter McArthur*, p. 209.)

7. *Friendly Acres*, p. 60.

8. *The Red Cow*, p. 210.

9. *Friendly Acres*, pp. 115–116.

10. *In Pastures Green*, p. 134.

11. The *Globe*, January 2, 1922, p. 37. *Friendly Acres*, p. 198.

12. *Friendly Acres*, pp. 196–197.

13. *The Red Cow*, pp. 282–283.

14. *In Pastures Green*, p. 143.

15. The *Globe*, December 10, 1910, p. 13. (*The Best of Peter McArthur*, p. 220.)

16. *In Pastures Green*, p. 240.

17. *The Red Cow*, p. 208.

18. *Ibid.*, p. 174.

19. *In Pastures Green*, p. 289.

20. *The Red Cow*, p. 230.

21. *Around Home*, p. 228.

22. *In Pastures Green*, p. 312.

23. The *Globe*, June 3, 1911, p. 16.

24. *Friendly Acres*, p. 86.

25. *Around Home*, p. 100.

26. *In Pastures Green*, p. 68. See p. 66 for other comments on Bergson.

27. *Friendly Acres*, p. 16.

28. *In Pastures Green*, p. 116.

29. *Friendly Acres*, pp. 13, 14.

30. The *Globe*, December 10, 1910, p. 13. (*The Best of Peter McArthur*, p. 181.)

31. *Ibid.*

32. *Friendly Acres*, p. 86.

33. The *Globe*, November 11, 1919, p. 7. (*The Best of Peter McArthur*, p. 255.)

34. The *Globe*, December 10, 1910, p. 13. (*The Best of Peter McArthur*, p. 221.)

35. *In Pastures Green*, p. 64.

36. *Friendly Acres*, p. 209.

37. *In Pastures Green*, p. 201.

38. *Ibid.*, p. 101.

39. Letter to Vaux, October 8, 1911.

40. "Country Observations," The *Globe*, April 25, 1914, p. 14.

41. *Around Home,* p. 64.

42. *In Pastures Green*, p. 87.

43. *Around Home*, p. 88.

44. "Setting Out," the *Globe*, October 4, 1913, p. 15. (*The Best of Peter McArthur*, p. 251.)

45. *Friendly Acres*, p. 151.

46. *In Pastures Green*, pp. 349–350.

47. *Ibid.*, p. 146.

48. *Around Home*, p. 85.

49. *Friendly Acres*, p. 161.

50. "The Pioneer Afoot," *Ourselves* I, 3 (December, 1910), p. 128.

51. *In Pastures Green*, p. 165.

52. *Ibid.*, p. 136. See also *Friendly Acres*, p. 141.

53. *Around Home*, p. 113.
54. *In Pastures Green*, 179.
55. *Around Home*, p. 75.
56. *The Affable Stranger*, p. 70.
57. *The Last Law—Brotherhood*, p. 20.
58. *Around Home* pp. 88–89.
59. "The Monthly Talk," *Ourselves*, I, 3 (December, 1910), p. 105.
60. "Reciprocity With Canada," *Forum*, XLIV, 6 (December, 1910), p. 662.
61. Letter to Vaux, March 29, 1912.
62. "The Canadian Banking Combine," *Ourselves*, I, 8 (April, 1912), p. 385.
63. *Ibid.*, pp. 374–375.
64. *In Pastures Green*, pp. 95, 96.
65. "Peter McArthur and the Agrarian Myth," *Queen's Quarterly*, 67, 2 (Summer, 1960), p. 254.
66. Letter to Vaux, February 13, 1920.
67. It was supposedly a study of the attitudes of the ordinary American citizens toward Canada when, after World War I, Canadians had developed a strong dislike of the United States. McArthur found that the people were little concerned with Canada and that any unfriendly feelings were mainly the result of the politically minded press.
68. *In Pastures Green*, p. x.
69. *The Affable Stranger*, pp. 68, 112.
70. *Ibid.*, p. 113.
71. *The Last Law—Brotherhood*, p. 13.
72. *The Affable Stranger*, p. 116.
73. *My Home* (Toronto: Whaley, Royce & Co., 1908).
74. *The Last Law—Brotherhood*, p. 56.
75. "The People's Editorial," *Ourselves*, I, 5 (February, 1911), p. 219.
76. *The Last Law—Brotherhood*, p. 38.
77. "Poetic News," the *Globe*, August 6, 1924, p. 4.
78. *Friendly Acres*, p. 97.
79. *The Sufficient Life*, pp. 9–10. McArthur papers, the University of Western Ontario.
80. *Around Home*, p. 22.
81. Manuscript, "Hyphenated Canadianism," p. 5.
82. *In Pastures Green*, p. 217.
83. *Ibid.*, p. 197.
84. *The Red Cow*, p. 83. See also *In Pastures Green*, p. 206.
85. *In Pastures Green*, p. 283.

86. *Ibid.,* p. 317.
87. *The Last Law—Brotherhood,* pp. 19, 54, 55.
88. *The Affable Stranger,* p. 73.
89. *In Pastures Green,* p. 3.
90. *Friendly Acres,* 204.

Selected Bibliography

PRIMARY SOURCES

1. Published Books

Five Sonnets. Privately printed, New York, 1899.

Lines. Privately printed, New York, 1901.

To Be Taken Wtih Salt: Being an Essay on Teaching One's Grand-mother to Suck Eggs. London: Limpus Baker & Co., 1903.

The Ghost and the Burglar. New York: McArthur and Ryder, 1905.

The Peacemakers. New York: McArthur and Ryder, 1905.

The Sufficient Life. New York: Long Island Loan and Trust Co., 1906.

The Prodigal and Other Poems. New York: Mitchell Kennerly, 1907.

In Pastures Green. London and Toronto: J. M. Dent & Sons, 1915.

The Red Cow and Her Friends. Toronto: J. M. Dent & Sons, 1919.

Sir Wilfrid Laurier. Toronto: J. M. Dent & Sons, 1919.

The Affable Stranger. Toronto: Thomas Allen, 1921.

The Last Law—Brotherhood. Toronto: Thomas Allen, 1921.

Stephen Leacock. Toronto: Ryerson Press, 1923.

Unselfish Money. Waterloo: Reinsurance Co., n.d.

The Deep Waters: Lighthouse Flashes. Waterloo. Ontario Equitable Life and Accident Insurance Co., n.d.

A Chant of Mammonism. Waterloo: Ontario Equitable Life and Accident Insurance Co., [1922].

The Anchor Post. Waterloo: Ontario Equitable Life and Accident Insurance Co., n.d.

The River of Gold. Waterloo: Ontario Equitable Life and Accident Insurance Co., n.d.

Good Measure. [Waterloo?]: Mutual Life Assurance Co., n.d.

Around Home. Toronto: Musson Book Co., 1925.

Familiar Fields. Toronto: J. M. Dent & Sons, 1925.

Friendly Acres. Toronto: Musson Book Co., 1927.

2. Published Articles

"Another 'Great Misunderstood.'" *Punch,* 123 (December 10, 1902), p. 401.

"Canada as she is Misunderstood." *Punch,* 123 (October 15, 1902), p. 259.

"Canadian Banking System." *Forum*, 50 (July, 1913), pp. 59–65.
"Defeat of Reciprocity." *Forum*, 46 (November, 1911), pp. 536–545.
"On Having Known A Poet." *Atlantic Monthly*, May, 1906, pp. 711–714.
"Reciprocity with Canada." *Forum*, 44 (December, 1910), pp. 655–662.
"Stubborn Farmer." *Forum*, 47 (March, 1912), pp. 337–343.
"The Canadian Banking Combine." *Ourselves*, I, 8 (April, 1912), pp. 361–391.

3. Main Unpublished Works

Prince Aguilar. A drama, c. 1898.
Cayuga Brook. A novel, c. 1900.
"Cosmic Consciousness." A long essay on Whitman and Richard M. Bucke, 1913.
The Unknown Soldier. A verse drama, 1924.

SECONDARY SOURCES

1. Books

DEACON, WILLIAM ARTHUR. *Peter McArthur.* Toronto: Ryerson Press, 1924. Written during McArthur's lifetime. Contains a short selection from McArthur's works. Places stress on serious poetry.

LUCAS, ALEC. *The Best of Peter McArthur.* Toronto: Clarke, Irwin & Co., 1967.

2. Articles

BRUCE, H. ADDINGTON. "Hard Knocks for an Optimist." *London Free Press*, December 3, 1966. p. 6-M.
————. "Hambidge, McArthur Team Breaks Up." *London Free Press*, December 10, 1966, p. 8-M. These articles describe McArthur's years in New York.

CONRON, BRANDON. "Essays (1880–1920)." In *Literary History of Canada.* Toronto: University of Toronto Press, 1965, pp. 340–346.

DEACON, WILLIAM ARTHUR. "A Living Voice." *Saturday Night*, November, 1924, pp. 1–2. A brief, but good, survey of McArthur's life and work.

DUFF, CLAYTON. "Browsings Among the Books." *Farmer's Advocate*, 50, 48 (December 2, 1915), pp. 1889–1890. A good study of *In Pastures Green.*

EGGLESTON, WILFRID. "The Causerie." *Winnipeg Free Press*, March 25, 1950, p. [19].

HATHAWAY, RUFUS H. "Vale! Peter McArthur," *Canadian Bookman*, 7, 1 (January, 1925), pp. 8, 12.

McNALLY, DAVID. "Peter McArthur and Canadian Nationalism." *Ontario History*, 69, 1 (March, 1972), pp. 1–10. Surveys the development of McArthur's nationalism as regards the United States and Britain.

MIDDLETON, J. E. "Peter McArthur." *Canadian Forum*, 5, 51 (December, 1924), pp. 82, 84–85.

WATT, F. W. "Peter McArthur and the Agrarian Myth." *Queen's Quarterly*, 67, 2 (Summer, 1960), pp. 245–257.

WELLS, KENNETH. "Introduction" to *In Pastures Green*. Toronto: J. M. Dent & Sons (Canada), 1948.

Index